Don't fuss, love God, don't fuss

Compiled by
Ruth A. Bamforth

Faithbuilders Publishing
12 Dukes Court, Bognor Road
Chichester, PO19 8FX, United Kingdom
www.faithbuilderspublishing.com

ISBN: 978-1-913181-68-0

Hymns Ancient and Modern Revised Edition

Photo credit: Pocklington Post and Roger Pattison

Cover by Esther Kotecha, EK Design
Layout by Faithbuilders Publishing
Printed in the United Kingdom

For Dad

1935 - 2015

Contents

Endorsements

A sermon is a very particular and personal thing, an exchange with one unique group of people at one unique time. As well as writing a record of her Father's long life, Ruth Bamforth has collected together a selection of his sermons. They will be an inspiration to many who are trying to inspire people with the Gospel message through their preaching.

Tony Robinson
Bishop of Wakefield

I am delighted to endorse Ruth's book about her Father, The Revd (Fr) Stuart Bamforth. I really got to know him and his wife when they were in Market Weighton, in retirement. It was very quickly apparent that here was a priest of deep faith, with an amazing understanding of vocation which never let him become proud or superior in faith but a man and a priest who "walked humbly before the God who had called him and who he followed in obedience". A pastor, an educator, a man of deep prayer, sensitive and a very genuine pastor. Many people, priests and students will always remember him as someone who delighted in them, listened to their needs and supported them through the ups and downs of life. What I said in my letter to him on the 50th Anniversary of his Ordination is still true. We rejoice in the memory of a faithful priest and pray: "Come ye blessed children of my Father, receive the kingdom prepared for you from the beginning of the world". May Fr Stuart truly Rest in Peace and Rise in Glory. Alleluia!

The Ven. Richard Seed
Former Archdeacon of York

Foreword

How do Christians learn to live Christ's Story in contemporary life? One key way is by reflecting with a mature and trusted fellow traveller about the journey, its opportunities and challenges, whilst on the road. *Don't Fuss, Love God, Don't Fuss,* compiled and edited by Ruth Bamforth in thanksgiving for her late father, Stuart, gives us an opportunity to see this approach to community formation and learning through the lens of Stuart Bamforth's many years of preaching sermons. Many of these were given during his time in the Diocese of York whilst he served in the Londesborough and the Holme on Spalding Moor groups of parishes. His passion in preaching was to seek answers to life's great questions and thereby enable ordinary Christians in the pews to benefit from the distilled learning and wisdom which he accrued over these years of ministry, much of which he got by listening to the stories and concerns of parishioners.

Reading his sermons I was struck by their down to earth character and their expansive range. You can imagine yourself listening and being helped and challenged by his insights into Scripture, reflected on within the Church as the community of the faithful set within an ever changing world. These sermons are theology on the go, spoken thoughts about the ways of God with us and with the world, as part of that unfolding story of faith in ordinary life consequent upon the impact of Jesus Christ over 2,000 years ago. They help us to imagine what it looks like to live Christ's Story in time and place as we seek to love God and be released from our own self-preoccupation.

Sermons inevitably have a date on them. They do not pretend to stand outside their context. However this does not mean that they cannot be re-contextualised in our own time and place. As we read them we hear an ancestor in the faith doing what all preachers are called to do, namely to share

Christ's meaning for us and for this world in local settings. In so doing we are helped to see ways we can do this in our related but different society. I hope you enjoy and are challenged by *Don't Fuss, Love God, Don't Fuss*.

Foreword by Dr John Thomson
Bishop of Selby, Diocese of York.

Preface

I am a pensions lawyer, not a theologian. My Dad was an Anglican priest. He had an amazing ability to preach and communicate. He knew what to say, when to say it and to whom. His vocation was his life. God was number one.

We were in a hospital side-room; Mum, Dad, my sister and I. Dad had died, or so we thought. He'd stopped breathing. His pulse ceased. He went grey. Silently we sat by his bed, not wanting to tell the nurses – yet.

Suddenly Dad took a deep breath and opened his eyes, "I'm back!" Back for good? Back to put things straight?

Nothing existed for us outside that hospital room. On and off Dad talked for twelve hours. I will never forget how he held my hand, looked at me intently, "I am so happy to have had you," he said. How in the middle of the night he turned to Mum, whose head was lolling as she catnapped in an upright chair, smiled sweetly and whispered, "I am so in love. I am not a handsome chap, but I am so in love". And that after fifty years of marriage!

Dad was on a road, a journey, his final journey – we, the five of us, were with him.

"But Dad, there are four of us, not five."

"There are five of us, I tell you – the Lord is with us," he insisted.

What more to say. We walked the long road – the five of us – through the darkest hours of that night: at times quietly, at times in agitation.

Around 5am a calm descended. Dad opened his eyes, "It is finished. Goodbye. Na-night". Dad never spoke another word.

For Dad, God was number one but we, his family, were never second best. Somehow Dad squared that impossible circle, but I do not know how.

Dad. Rest in peace.

Introduction

"The ultimate test of worth and value of a person is not how much we know: it is the test of how we answer the great questions of life, the great challenges, what reply we make."[1]

The modern world in which we live today is hectic and fast paced. The day to day lives for most of us seem to be unbearably frenetic as we attempt (with a greater or lesser degree of success) to juggle our work and home lives. It is important, therefore, for each and every one of us regularly to find a quiet space to take stock and consider where we are on our journey as a follower of Christ – whether we are at the beginning of our journey or whether we have been walking the path of faith for many years.

Much has been written about what it means to be a Christian. This is especially true in today's world when there are many different methods of communication and approaches to learning, whether from books or online interactive tools. Whatever the latest modern method of communicating, when it comes to exploring our faith we can still learn from clear and concise explanations of what it means to be a Christian no matter when they were expressed, whether recently or many years ago.

Stuart Michael Bamforth was my Dad. At Dad's request we marked his life and passing with a Requiem Mass. He left clear instructions dealing with every aspect of the service. He chose the hymns and the form of the liturgy. He also stipulated that there be a short homily on the sacrament of the priesthood, "that to which I have given so much of my life".

At his death Dad had been an Anglican priest for more than 52 years. Not only that, but Dad had been active in his Christian ministry from the time of his ordination until his

---

[1] Extract from a sermon preached at St John Baptist, Adel, Advent 4 1995

13

final illness. Dad died in December 2015. However, to this day Dad is fondly remembered by many of those whose path he crossed, not only as a man and a priest but also for his ability to communicate clearly and memorably the Christian message.

The following chapters of this book are a selection of Dad's sermons which I have edited into a series of thought pieces which consider important issues such as, what is a Christian and how to pray, as well as the meaning and importance of the sacraments. These thought pieces express the Christian message in which Dad believed and which he taught. I would like to think also that something of my Dad's personality is revealed through them. At the end of each chapter there are some questions for you to consider. Before you read the rest of this book, in this chapter I would like to share something of my Dad's life-story, to put his work in context and to explain the impact he made, and continues to make, on those he came into contact with. Most importantly I would like to share something of how my Dad practiced what he preached, how he strived to live his life as a follower of Christ.

Dad was the long-awaited only child of Gladys and Raymond Bamforth of Hoyland near Barnsley in South Yorkshire. He was born at home on 30 April 1935 which was, according to Grandma, a gloriously sunny day.

Grandpa and Grandma were ordinary and straightforward people. Grandpa had left school at 13 and had gone to work in a Barnsley British Co-operative Society grocery shop as the flour boy. Other than during World War 2, Grandpa worked for the Co-op all his life, eventually retiring as a shop manager. When Grandma left school, she worked as a parlour maid in Sheffield. She always joked that she never got her hands dirty until she married Grandpa. As was typical at the time (Grandpa and Grandma got married in 1929) Grandma gave up work when she married. Or at least Grandma gave up paid work, she worked tirelessly to support Grandpa to increase the business of whatever Co-op shop he was working in. They were a real team.

Dad grew up in a kind, loving and supportive family which encouraged his natural curiosity. When he was a very little boy, because Dad was always wanting to "help", Grandpa gave him a small square of garden as his own. Dad was very keen to look after his plants. The only problem was that he kept pulling them up – just to check what they were doing. It is probably no surprise that Dad's plants did not do well.

Grandad Young (Grandma's father) was a key figure in Dad's childhood, and they were close until his death in 1965. Grandpa was called up to serve in the RAF on American Independence Day 1940 – he was one of the oldest to be conscripted, born as he was in 1905. That left Grandma having to deal with the worry of Grandpa being away and to bring up Dad who was aged only five. Grandad Young stepped into the breach. He spent a lot of time with his live-wire grandson who simply couldn't stop asking questions and pushing the boundaries.

On one occasion Dad asked, "Can I have a swear Grandad?" "Yes," said Grandad Young, "but make sure your mother doesn't find out" – swearing to Grandma was a total no no. Grandad Young realised that a little boy whose father had gone to war needed to let off steam. On another occasion, Dad's school was offering a chocolate bar to the child who could collect and name the most wild flowers. When Dad told Grandad Young, Grandad Young told him not to worry he would get the prize. So, the two of them went out collecting and, sure enough, Dad won the prize which Grandad Young insisted that he did not share.

There are many little stories I could relate about Dad as a child. Grandma enjoyed telling my sister Rachel and I what Dad had done, possibly when she thought he and Mum were being somewhat too strict with us. One final story I would like to share of Dad's early childhood occurred when he was around eight or nine years old. Dad's class went on a school trip. The teacher, Miss Guest, had given the class a long list of dos and don'ts. Dad decided that he wished to have an ice-cream.

Dad checked the list and then bought one. Miss Guest saw Dad eating the ice-cream and took him to task. She was not best pleased when Dad replied quite politely but firmly, "But Miss Guest, you didn't say that we couldn't have an ice-cream". He was right, ice-cream was not on the list.

Grandpa and Grandma were not regular worshippers and church was never a prominent part of Dad's childhood. Grandpa had been confirmed into the Anglican Church as a child, but Grandma was not confirmed until after Mum and Dad were married. In fact, in one sermon from 1965 Dad mentions that Grandma suggested that they should go to church to thank God for Dad's recovery from a severe illness. Dad commented that neither he nor Grandma felt at ease in the church and that he remembered that he could almost smell the cold dampness of the building as they knelt to pray.

Grandma and Grandpa were quietly very proud of their son. They believed strongly that it was not good to boast. This meant that they did not broadcast Dad's academic and other achievements to the world. They realised that Dad would have succeeded at whatever he turned his hand to. That said, they were always there to support their son.

At the end of Dad's first term in the sixth form he decided that he wanted to drop the sciences in favour of Latin and Greek. Grandpa and Grandma were called up to school as a result. They supported Dad's decision, despite the fact that Dad would not be given any help to catch up and the fact that they had hoped that Dad would have gone into medicine. In fact, when Dad decided to become a priest, he told his parents that he would be a "doctor of souls".

Dad first met John Bilton in 1949 when he transferred to Barnsley Grammar School from Ecclesfield Grammar School. However, because Dad and John were in different classes it was not until they were in the sixth form (1951-54) that their life-long friendship began. John told me that in the sixth form boys needed to choose between the arts and the sciences. In addition, sixth form study focussed primarily upon what was known about a subject. Most of their contemporaries were happy with this approach but not Dad and John. They had interests across the arts/sciences divide, even though Dad was studying classics and John music. They were both keen to search for a more unified way of thinking than that offered by the school's more polarised approach.

John recalled that there was a natural intellectual combustion to their friendship. Neither was afraid to talk about subjects seriously, but always with good humour. As John said in a letter to me after Dad's death, "we developed our intellectual and spiritual outlooks together, each of us sharpening the cutting edge of effective engagement by supporting and questioning each other's values and beliefs. Even when we reached different conclusions, the rock of our friendship never faltered."

John was a regular church-goer in the Anglo-Catholic tradition. John's parish priest had introduced him as a teenager to Nashdom, the Anglican Benedictine monastery in Buckinghamshire. Nashdom at the time was a vibrant community of around thirty professed monks. One monk in particular stood out, Dom Robert Petitpierre.

Dom Robert came from a wealthy family (originally Swiss) who had a number of business interests. He was a polymath who, before he became a monk in middle-age, kept a hand in the family business as well as lecturing in chemistry at St Bede's College, Durham. According to John he was a good theologian but yet had his feet very much on the ground.

Dom Robert was a gifted communicator and analyser of situations. He was the type of person that once you had met him you would not forget him. Dom Robert was also someone who enjoyed keeping in touch with people and had an unerring ability to know exactly when a letter or a phone call was needed.

John took Dad to Nashdom for a long-weekend stay in 1953. John had no idea when he took Dad for the visit what its outcome would be but "the testimony to that visit became his life's work, symbolised many years later in his choice of

"Nashdom" as the name of his retirement home". One thing John did know was that Dad was very taken with the Nashdom liturgy (in Latin) and that he was attracted to Nashdom's ordered sense of Christianity rather than, as John put it, the "messy explosion of evangelicalism". John also thought that Dad's one to one chat and subsequent correspondence with Dom Robert (who became Dad's spiritual adviser) may have sparked something off.

After the Nashdom trip, the nature of some of Dad and John's discussions changed. Many of their earlier discussions asked questions such as, "why did the industrial revolution cause so much ugliness?" A discussion which was underpinned by a strong sense of morality. Later discussions asked questions such as, "are you a believer?" John believed that as time went on Dad began to ask himself whether *he* was a believer. Precisely when and where Dad went on to answer, "yes", to the question, "do you want to be ordained?" John did not know. Dad did not discuss the issue with him. Dad told John as a fait accompli. However, John was aware that Dad had a conviction that prayer was not an empty form of words and that it was possible to have truth revealed through prayer. John believed that Dad applied this conviction to his own life which led to the revelation that he should be ordained.

When Dad was at school the Oxford entrance exam was taken in the term after A level results. A school scholarship enabled Dad to spend the summer in which he sat his A levels and the following summer before he went up to Oxford in Italy learning Italian. Dad had originally expected to go to Italy one year and Greece the next but the Greek crisis over Cyprus meant that a trip to Greece was impossible.

As far as I can tell from what Dad said, he was unphased at the thought of crossing Europe on a train and having little means of contacting home once he arrived. Grandpa and Grandma were worried, however. The original arrangements were that Dad was to stay at a convent in Rome – the Italian language school had not realised that

Stuart was a boy's name. Obviously an 18-year-old boy could not stay in a convent. Grandma had a friend who had kept in touch with a former prisoner of war. The plan was that Dad would stay with this family. The only problem was that Grandma had not received a letter confirming arrangements by the time that Dad had to set off.

Dad loved his time in Rome and became a great Italophile. He excelled at the Italian language and ended up a fluent speaker. He also spent a lot of time exploring the historical and artistic wonders of Rome. The second year Dad went he spent the summer helping Guido, the son of a prominent judge and about Dad's age, with his English. Dad had a great time with Guido sailing the family's yacht and riding around on a vespa. Dad's Italian improved more than Guido's English, however. Guido was more interested in chasing girls than studying.

Dad went up to Hertford College, Oxford as a state scholar where he read Greats (classics, ancient history and philosophy) between 1954 and 1958. Ian Donaldson, a friend from Hertford College, recalls that the 1954 intake of scholars were nearly all put on one staircase - N.B.6. Dad and Geoffrey Steeley (another friend) had rooms on the ground floor. Dad's set had a biggish sitting room overlooking the quad, which meant he could see what was going on and Ian and the others could see if he was in or not. As a result, Ian said that, "there was a tendency to drop in as one passed by".

The scholars sat at a special table at dinner and the "new boys" sat at the bottom of the table (at least for the first term). This seating arrangement meant that Dad, Ian, Geoffrey and the others left dinner together and, if they were not doing other things, they would often end up in Dad's rooms solving the problems of the world or probably much more mundane matters. Ian remembered that Dad was always polite, friendly and vaguely hospitable, although he did think from time to time that Dad would rather his "guests" would just go.

Several of the scholars were fairly frequent chapel attenders, said Evensong at 6.30pm immediately before dinner was semi-compulsory for the first years. The Hertford Chapel was low church, and the chaplain was ex-RAF with a particular concentration on the "Word". Ian said that he, Dad and many of the other attendees enjoyed the Book of Common Prayer's cadences rather than what was preached there.

Dad's intellectual sparring partner at Oxford was Geoffrey Steeley. Geoffrey recalled that Dad had a great spark as well as a great intellect. They spent a lot of time together discussing issues, as well as the derivation and hidden meaning of words. Geoffrey was much more of a free thinker whose mind jumped around. Dad, on the other hand, liked order and reason.

Geoffrey remembered that the first time he met Dad, Dad already identified himself as being intrinsically religious. This was despite the fact that Dad was not actually confirmed into the Church of England when he went up to Oxford. As Dad himself put it in a sermon from 1965:

"[W]hen the evening came during my first year at university on which I came to know that I had to offer myself for confirmation I had no other thought in my head but the fact that God himself had spoken to me and moved me."

During most of his time in Oxford Dad attended Pusey House. Pusey House was (and still is) in the Anglo-Catholic tradition of the Church of England. Before finding Pusey House, Dad had tried various other forms of worship. Initially Dad attended many evangelical study groups and prayer meetings. He also recalled attending an open-air service on the Cowley towpath. Dad said that he felt sorry for the harangued people of Cowley and never went to an open-air service again. A friend then took Dad to solemn high Mass at Pusey House. With that visit Dad realised that he had found his spiritual home. Geoffrey recognised this when he told me that the form of worship at Pusey House satisfied something in Dad's soul.

During Dad's time at Oxford he continued to visit Nashdom. Geoffrey and some of Dad's other friends sometimes went with him. Just as John Bilton had realised when he took Dad to Nashdom for the first time, Geoffrey saw that Nashdom made a great impact on Dad. Geoffrey thought that this might be because at Nashdom there was a great emphasis on being human. It was not enough simply to be religious even though there was, at the same time, a great emphasis on structure. Dad's visits to Nashdom led him to being gently teased about becoming a monk. Ian recalled that the problem was that in denying it Dad looked rather like a monk.

The crunch time for Dad at Oxford was his illness. I am not sure what was wrong with him, although John Bilton thought that Dad had contracted a virus during the time he spent in Italy. Whatever the cause, the illness was serious and life-threatening. I remember Dad saying to me that he heard a nurse outside his door asking someone to be quiet because, "there is a boy in there dying". Dad said that he looked round the room and he was alone: a sobering realisation indeed. Dad's parents were asked if they would consent to Dad being given an experimental treatment in order to try to save his life. They agreed. It worked but at a terrible cost. The life-saving streptomycin was given orally rather than by injection. It seriously damaged Dad's hearing.

In the 1950s disability was not as accepted as it is today. Dad's deafness was initially spasmodic and undiagnosed. This led initially to the thought that Dad was just not up to the mark academically. However, Dad's diagnosis coincided with him losing his hearing rapidly. Dad was not totally deaf, but he had lost sufficient hearing to struggle considerably in day-to-day life and to require a hearing aid. Mum learnt the story of what happened next from Dad's parents.

Dad had lodgings in Oxford with some friends of his parents. On the day Dad discovered that he was deaf he went back to his digs and went to his room. His landlord and landlady went to Dad's door and heard him sobbing his heart out. They crept downstairs not feeling that they could intrude on Dad's grief and waited until Dad appeared. Eventually Dad came downstairs. He was dry-eyed and he never once mentioned to them that he was deaf. Indeed, to the day he died he refused to accept that he was disabled.

Geoffrey also remembered that Dad reacted by hiding himself away to work. Most of Dad's Oxford friends did not know how to help him. Geoffrey and another friend, Ian Scargill, paced their speech slowly so that Dad could follow them. Dad's deafness was hardest in social situations. He had to work hard at communicating and, instead of his previous conversational quickness, he would often only say something when he considered it important.

Dad's illness and resulting deafness impacted his studies. John Bilton told me that the consequence of this was that the idea of becoming an Oxford don (an aspiration Dad had had since schooldays) was pushed out of Dad's mind and was replaced with a very different kind of vocation – the priesthood. John considered that being a priest used more of Dad's natural abilities and resources. John said that Dad had a greater range of influence and expression than he would have had if he had become an Oxford don.

The Church authorities considered that potential ordinands should have experience of ordinary life and ordinary people before ordination. This meant that Dad had a two-year wait after Oxford before he could go to theological college in Salisbury. The fact that Dad was from a down to earth, working class family did not make any difference. Dad spent this two years from 1958 to 1960 in Slough in Buckinghamshire.

For the first six months Dad worked in an asbestos factory on the Slough industrial estate. After four years at university, he did not find working in a factory easy – clocking in at 7:45 every morning, a 15 minute morning break, three quarters of an hour for lunch, a five minute tea break in the afternoon, before clocking off at 5:30. Dad also said that management had made his time in the factory a bit harder. They let it be known that Dad was going to be ordained to the priesthood. That knowledge put many of the factory workers off Dad even though some of them did ask him some serious questions about God and the Church.

After he left the factory, for the rest of Dad's two years in Slough he taught Latin at a small preparatory school. Dad did such a good job of not only teaching but also running the school that the lady who owned the school wanted to give the school to him.

During his time in Slough, Dad worshiped at the Slough trading estate church of St Michael and All Angels. Father John Room, who later became one of the Church of England's senior and most experienced industrial chaplains, was the priest in charge. When Dad knew him, Father John was beginning to make St Michael's the springboard for outreach into the industrial world of the many factories on the trading estate. This example of outreach made a great impression on Dad. Indeed, such outreach formed an important part of Dad's ministry as both an incumbent in Norfolk and during his years of teaching.

Dad went to Salisbury Theological College where, in his second and final year, he was the Senior Student. He had originally intended to go to Chichester but had been told that all was not well there (I do not know what the issue was). When Dad was at Salisbury the Principal was Freddie Tindall and the Vice Principal (known to everyone as Vice) was George Thompson. Dad had a lot of time for the Principal. He thought he was an able theologian who was full of insights, one in particular being the importance of community or fellowship regardless of the matter under discussion. Vice was a precise man of small stature who wrote commentaries on the Gospels. He and Dad became great friends and indeed he was to be my godfather.

Salisbury Theological College was run on monastic lines. The Great Silence was observed each day and there were regular college retreats. It was during these retreats that Dad first learned the value of silence and of listening.

Dad recalled in one sermon in 2009 that college had been in retreat from first thing on Monday morning to first thing on Saturday morning. During that time the students were required to attend several services each day in chapel, listen to devotional addresses and not to talk at all, except to say "please pass the salt", or whatever at meal times. The retreat ended after Mass on Saturday morning. Dad took his breakfast on the Vice Principal's table. "Good morning, Stuart," he said, "and how are you?" "Amazed," Dad replied. "I haven't heard anything said that was worth breaking the silence for." Dad remembered that the Vice Principal smiled at the truth of what he said. Although Dad did comment in his sermon, "What a bumptious young man I was!"

That said, Dad learnt the listening lesson well. He felt that his years in parish life taught him that it was far more important to listen than to speak. Dad was sure that listening first to what his parishioners had to say helped him give them more realistic advice. In fact, since Dad has died one of the comments which has been made about him on so many occasions was his great skill as a listener and adviser.

Not all the students appreciated the monastic regime at Salisbury, however. One evening, Vice told Mum, after the start of the Great Silence, the sounds of banging doors could be heard throughout the college. The banging was accompanied by a crescendo of noise. Vice went to Dad's room just as Dad had expected. Vice was all for bringing the culprits, whoever they were, to book for unbecoming conduct. Dad's response was that confrontation was exactly what the men were looking for. Instead, Dad suggested that Vice did not rise to the bait. After much persuasion Vice agreed and, eventually, the cacophony of noise subsided and the college corridors were again silent. The next morning at breakfast everyone expected something would be said. Vice said nothing. No further disturbance of the Great Silence occurred. Dad's quiet but shrewd reading of the situation had ensured that trouble was averted.

In many ways one of the key events of Dad's life occurred when he was at Salisbury: his cousin Sheena introduced him to Mum. Mum and Sheena met when they were studying to become special needs teachers in

Manchester. Sheena thought that Mum and Dad would hit it off and so played matchmaker.

Mum and Dad's first meeting did not have a particularly auspicious start. Sheena and Mum were to meet Dad at the bus station, but they were late. Dad was not in the best of moods when Sheena and Mum turned up. His opening gambit was that he had been about to get on the next bus back to Barnsley.

After many apologies, as a result of which Mum and Sheena's lateness was forgotten, they eventually ended up at the small flat which Mum and Sheena shared for lunch. Lunch was to be a mixed grill cooked on a tiny Baby Belling stove. Mum was in charge of the cooking. Dad was propping the door up. Mum became rather flustered (she was not yet the amazing cook she is today) and so she asked Dad if he would like to go into the other room. No, was Dad's reply, I am fine here. It was only in retrospect that Mum realised that she had asked Dad the wrong question.

After lunch, at Sheena's suggestion, Mum and Dad went for a walk in the local park. Mum said that they had a lovely stroll in the sunshine and ended up sitting on a park bench. Somehow the conversation turned to church matters and the pros and cons of infant baptism. Dad was not in favour of infant baptism, a person should be baptised at the same time as confirmation to candidates who desire it[2]. Mum disagreed. Fairly recently Mum related this story to Dad's friend John. John was astounded that Mum had had the temerity to take Dad on in a theological debate. Mum's response was that she had never had to work so hard in her life to justify the position she was holding.

It might not have been the most conventional start to a relationship but at Dad's death Mum and Dad had been married for just over fifty very happy years. I think it is a great testament to the strength of the bond they had together that they were happiest in each other's company. Their personalities complimented each other, and they were

---

[2] See p130 for Dad's explanation of his views on infant baptism.

always there for the other to lean on. As Dad once said, he could cope with any difficulties in life because he could return to the calm and happy home that he and Mum had made.

Dad was ordained deacon at Ripon Cathedral by the then Bishop of Ripon, John Moorman, on Trinity Sunday 1962 and then priested at Ripon in 1963. After being deaconed, Dad became the first curate of St John Baptist, Adel in Leeds. Canon Philip Simpson, one of the most senior priests in the diocese and a trusted adviser and close confidant to the Bishop, was the Rector of Adel (and the sister church at Ireland Wood) under whom Dad was to serve his title.

Philip was a good theologian and a bit of a stickler. He expected that all his curates (Dad was one of four, though the others were based at Ireland Wood) had to attend every service without fail. Philip also vetted every sermon to be preached by his deacon curates. I do not know whether or not Dad ever had to make any changes to the sermons he wished to preach. That said, Dad was nicknamed, "Collect man", by his fellow curates because for a whole year each sermon he preached was on the collect for the day.

During Dad's curacy he was the chaplain to East Moor Approved School, a reform school in the Adel parish for boys aged between thirteen and nineteen. As well as his other duties, Dad spent each Tuesday evening at East Moor getting to know both the boys and the staff. Dad was not a somewhat remote figure who only lectured the boys on moral and religious matters. In fact, one of the first things Dad did was to start up a badminton club in the school and, once the boys could play to a reasonable standard, Dad persuaded local badminton groups to challenge the boys to a game or two.

Dad kept around fifty of the sermons which he preached to the East Moor boys. It is striking Dad did not talk down to the boys. In fact the opposite was true. He certainly talked to the boys about the importance of God and wider morality, but in the majority of cases he seems to have tried to do this in language which they would easily understand. One sermon from 1964 stands out in particular.

Dad was preaching on the subject of God as "Our Father". He told the boys that when he went to Oxford, he knew he had two sides to himself: a good side and a bad side, like everyone else. One day Dad became fed up with the bad side and tried to do something about it on his own. Then Dad was introduced to Jesus. Dad found out that Jesus had opened an everlasting telephone call to God so that Dad could always get through to God and be listened to and taken care of. Jesus laid down one condition about Dad using him to get through to God, that Dad became a member of the Church, "a member of God's gang".

I have no idea what impression Dad made on the East Moor boys in the long term. However, it is true to say that Dad made something of an impression on at least one young person from Adel which has lasted until today. Bob Holloway, a teenager when Dad was a curate, remembers commenting to Dad that he had opened the Bible on the lectern for the appropriate Evensong readings. Dad replied, "Robert, in the Church of England we do not have readings, we have Lessons." A lesson which Bob says he has never forgotten.

In May 1967 Mum and Dad (they had married in September 1965) left Adel for Norfolk where Dad was going to have the livings of Hempton with Pudding Norton, Shereford and Toftrees as well as being priest in charge of Pensthorpe.

Mum and Dad enjoyed their time in Norfolk but Dad's job in Hempton in particular turned out to be much more challenging than he had initially been led to believe.

A week after Dad had been instituted, he and Mum were summoned to lunch with Lancelot Fleming, the Bishop of Norwich, and his wife. It was unusual for a new incumbent to be invited to lunch with the diocesan Bishop so quickly. When lunch was over, Dad was taken into the Bishop's study and the whole truth about the Hempton situation was revealed to him. In summary, Dad's (deceased) predecessor had allowed the parish to be run by a particular faction and there had been serious financial mismanagement. In fact, one day Dad received a final demand for repayment of a loan which no one other than his predecessor and the treasurer knew about. Dad always said that if he had been told the truth from the start, he would never have agreed to go to Hempton.

Dad did not have an easy ride cleaning up Hempton. The ring-leader of the faction was determined to do all that he could to stand in Dad's way, including by making life as difficult as he could for Mum. As Dad put it in a sermon in 2009:

"You have probably realised by now that when I preach I usually have a fairly full set of notes before me, or even a complete manuscript. Only once have I preached without either.

I was in Norfolk, in charge of five parishes and three churches. Four of the parishes and two of the churches were delightful, easy to get on with and full of Christian spirit.
The fifth parish, [Hempton] was the largest in terms of size and number of inhabitants. It was also, unfortunately for me, the place where my vicarage was – unfortunately, because it was a very difficult parish. So many members of the [Hempton] congregation had so little Christian spirit – they argued and quarrelled among themselves and enjoyed saying nasty things about me to my wife.

[One] year I could stand it no longer. We were celebrating the feast of the Epiphany. The Book of Common Prayer subtitles the Epiphany as the manifestation or showing of Christ to the Gentiles. Without notes I talked about the wise men from the east who had come to worship the newborn king. They had followed the message of a star and had to come great distances to worship the Messiah. I asked the congregation to ask themselves what sort of message their behaviour was sending to those outside the congregation – more than one of the "outsiders" had expressed sympathy for me in my difficulties."

Dad did eventually sort out the problems in Hempton and the parish was put back onto an even keel. Hempton, however, did not take up all of Dad's time in Norfolk. Dad played an active part in each of his parishes. As well as Sunday and weekday services in Hempton, Dad made sure that each of his other churches had at least a Sunday service each week. Dad had to have his timings perfect to make sure that he left one church to get to the next without being late. As Mum (who accompanied Dad to all the services) says, it is probably a good job that there was not too much traffic on the Norfolk lanes!

I think that Dad's approach to his parish ministry is summed up in his Hempton farewell speech on 10 October 1971:

"The first time I formally addressed parishioners of Hempton – in the marquee after the Institution and Induction – I said that I would be brief because I didn't wish to become known as one of those parsons who does not know when to stop talking…. Today, however, you may perhaps forgive me if I say more to you than I did on that first occasion nearly four and a half years ago.

As I thank you for your generosity and good wishes, I would like to mention one or two principles that I have constantly had before me as your parish priest. First of all, I have tried as far as possible to treat you all alike in the running of the Church to have no favourites, because I believe with all my mind that each and every member of our Church family has his/her own part to play, a part no one else can play, a part that is neither more nor less valuable than anybody else's.

Secondly, you all know that I have never tried to be popular. Perhaps life would have been easier for me in some ways if I had. But believing, as I have just said, in the unique value of every single member of our Church family, I have constantly tried, though God knows, with many a failure on my own part, to lead you all to God though the preaching of the Word and the Administration of the Sacraments, two of the chief duties lain upon a priest at his ordination. Whatever else may have happened, therefore, during our four and a half years association together, as priest and people, I hope that this at least may be said about me after I am gone: there was one thing about Father Bamforth, he did try to be faithful in preaching the Word and administering the Sacraments.

Well, the time is almost here for me to be gone – or, I should say, for us to be gone, because, whether you realise it or not, my wife has been a great and tremendous help to me during my incumbency. Perhaps she may not always have done all that some expected of her but at least she has done her best to keep me happy and well-fed – two chief tasks of a vicar's wife: indeed, of any wife, I would say!

And now, as I said when I left the parish in which I served my title, I will not say goodbye. Although I know well what it means – God be with you – yet it has come to have such a final ring about it. And who knows? We may yet be back in Norfolk again, if not to live, at least on holiday. When we shall hope to see you again.... Thank you so much. God bless you all."

The Church of England selection board who had put Dad forward for ordination had suggested to him that he had talents which they thought he should use in the community. They felt that Dad would not be able to use these talents to their full potential within the parish ministry. After leaving Norfolk, Dad followed the selection board's advice and went into teaching. Dad completed his teacher training in Oxford and then spent the rest of his time in paid employment teaching first in Nottingham and then in Leeds.

Dad initially taught RE at a comprehensive school in Nottingham. Dad found it a disillusioning experience. As he put it in 1995:

"My disillusionment was not surprising. I'd been teaching 33 lessons out of the 40-lesson week, meeting a different class each lesson; and each class had more than 30 pupils in it. I'd been prepared for lack of interest in my subject but lack of interest, hostility even, from so many, week in, week out, wore me down, despite all my efforts....

I was certainly in demand on parents' evenings, I would be one of the last teachers to leave, having spent as much of the evening in discussion of family problems as a whole as I did talking about my pupils."

After three difficult years Dad got a job in Leeds at Ralph Thoresby High School, a relatively newly opened comprehensive school. Mum had encouraged Dad to apply for the job even though it was not promotion, and they would have to make a costly house move. Dad spent the rest of his teaching career at Ralph Thoresby teaching Latin and English mainly, with some study skills and a little RE, as well as organising a great deal of community work.

Ralph Thoresby, although a comprehensive, was a very different type of school to the one Dad taught in Nottingham. Dawn Lynes, Ralph Thoresby's headmistress, was a gifted educationalist who believed in providing a rounded education for pupils whilst encouraging them to pursue their strengths. Dawn was also a devout Methodist who wanted Ralph Thoresby, which was not a faith school, to have a strong Christian ethos. One way in which Dawn did this was to take Dad up on the suggestion that the school hold a service each year in Holy Week. Dad led many of the services, but he also invited priests or ministers from different denominations to be involved.

I think that Dad, despite the inevitable frustrations, as a whole enjoyed his time teaching in Leeds. He was a strict disciplinarian who had a talent for inspiring his pupils. When I was a very junior barrister in the late 1990s, I took Mum and Dad to a formal dinner at Lincoln's Inn, my Inn of Court. After dinner Mum and I thought that Dad was taking an inordinate amount of time to collect his coat from the gentlemen's cloakroom. Finally, Dad reappeared talking to a student barrister. It turned out that Dad had taught the student (who was also an aspiring writer). The student had introduced Dad to his fellow students as, "This is Mr Bamforth who taught me all I know about the English language in his Latin classes."

Even though Dad earned his living as a teacher he was very much, as he put it, a schoolmaster in holy orders. During the whole time that Dad was teaching, and also after his retirement, he remained active in the Church ministry – certainly my sister and I felt that we were seen as the "daughters of the vicarage" even if that was not technically the case. When Dad was teaching in Nottingham the incumbent of St Lawrence's, Long Eaton was seriously ill and so Dad stepped in to take the Sunday services. We moved back to Adel, Leeds when I was three. My earliest church memories are of Dad celebrating the 8am Eucharist at Adel Church. In fact, during the 24 years Mum and Dad were in Adel, Dad had an altar each week whether at Adel or one of the other Leeds churches.

In 2000 Mum and Dad left Adel in Leeds and retired to Market Weighton on the edge of the Yorkshire Wolds. Almost as soon as they arrived Dad was assisting various incumbents in the local parishes and getting to know the local people.

Dad met Shelagh Jones in 2003 when she was a curate in the Londesborough group of parishes. In 2003, the Londesborough group was in the middle of an inter-regnum and Shelagh was getting much of her curacy supervision from a priest in another parish. Shelagh said that Dad was a great help to her during her training, despite the fact that she was sure that at the time Dad was a not a great supporter of the ordination of women priests.

In particular, Dad was able to tell Shelagh the technical names for everything that is put on the altar for the Eucharist as well as how to set the altar up correctly. Dad insisted that the veil on the chalice always had crisp corners and that the corporal was folded properly. When Shelagh said to Dad on one occasion that she was struggling with the corporal because it had been ironed the wrong way, Dad's immediate response was, "You must ask them to iron it correctly."

Shelagh told me that she did not always take Dad's advice, but she made sure that she gave Dad the reason why, which he appreciated. On one occasion, Shelagh and Dad were discussing whether or not the priest should face the congregation when singing the hymns. Shelagh said that she felt that she ought to turn to face the people to be part of the congregation. Dad's response was, "Shelagh, you are the priest, you are not part of the congregation. As the priest you should not turn to face the people during the hymns". Even though Shelagh told me that she does turn to face the congregation to sing the hymns, she can still hear Dad's voice in her head telling her not to do it.

Shelagh also recalled talking to Dad about prayers of intercession. Dad was clear that intercessions should not be too lengthy, but at the same time that it was important to give people the time to think and engage with each prayer.

Dad was a stickler for correctness. Shelagh said that Dad was due to take the Shiptonthorpe Holy Communion one St Bartholomew's day. The church had been prepared in green for the service before Dad arrived. Shelagh said that Dad swept into the church and walked purposefully up the aisle towards the vestry. Without a pause in his stride Dad announced, "St Bartholomew's day is red." No one said anything but they changed the colour to red to celebrate a saint's day. Shelagh thought that as a result of his comment Dad would preach on St Bartholomew. He didn't.

On the topic of Dad's sermons, Shelagh said that the congregation had to listen very carefully in order to follow the argument but that it was always worth the effort to listen. Shelagh also commented that she was always intrigued by the way in which he wove biographical details into his sermons. These details did not merely make a pleasant introduction, instead Shelagh felt that Dad used suitable biographical details to draw out the theological point he wished to make.

Shelagh said that Dad had a lovely but rather formal way with people. She said that it wasn't until after Dad stopped helping in the Londesborough group that she discovered that Dad had a wicked sense of humour. That said, Shelagh commented that Dad enjoyed getting to know and spending time talking to the people in the Londesborough group. For

Shelagh, Dad was a godsend during the inter-regnum. He kept the parishes organised and nurtured. Dad was the calming influence which was needed in order to overcome many of the problems which had beset the Londesborough group.

Shelagh felt that it was a real shame that the group's new incumbent did not appreciate the work which Dad had done in the group during the inter-regnum and did not want Dad's continued involvement. When the new incumbent told Shelagh (out of the blue) that he did not want her to continue with much of the work which she had been doing, he said that Stuart Bamforth had had the same devastated reaction to the news. Dad never mentioned this conversation to Shelagh, or as far as Shelagh is aware, to anyone else.

Shelagh is not the only person to comment that Dad had a rather formal way with people at first. In fact, the churchwarden at Market Weighton said that she was frightened of Dad until she got to know him better, he was so stern. Steve Smith, the Bielby churchwarden was another person who was initially apprehensive of Dad.

Steve and his fellow churchwarden had not had any training how to prepare the altar for the Eucharist. Steve realised quickly that Dad expected things to be done with precision and accuracy. Everything had to be just so. Steve really wanted to set the altar up properly, but he kept making small mistakes. One Sunday, Steve again did not quite get it right. Steve remembered that Dad pointed out the fault but with a small smile. Steve immediately relaxed. With that smile Steve knew that Dad understood he was trying to set the altar up correctly and Dad wanted to reassure him. Steve said that Dad's insistence on accuracy was done with empathy and understanding.

Steve told me that he took great comfort from Dad's care. For Steve, Dad was at peace with himself, and it was this inner peace which allowed Dad to care for others. However, Steve was clear that the care Dad showed was without compromise to his expectations. Steve told me the following story which illustrates Dad's approach.

Steve and his wife hosted a cheese and wine party at their house to raise funds for the church. Tickets were £15 with an additional £2 for each extra glass of wine. One man became rather drunk. The more he drank the louder he became and the more strident the views he expressed on the church. Steve was concerned about the situation. He also dreaded Dad coming into the kitchen and meeting the man.

Of course, the inevitable happened. Dad went into the kitchen and met the man. Steve said he marveled at the way in which Dad handled the situation. Immediately Dad took in what was going on and diffused the situation with humour and understanding. Dad made his views clear but not, Steve said, in an aggressive way. Dad sorted things out by defending the position of the church rather than trying to defend himself or his authority.

Seaton Ross was another village in the Holme-on-Spalding-Moor group with Bielby. When Dad knew it Seaton Ross was a very traditional congregation which used as its liturgy the 1662 Book of Common Prayer. Dave Raffaelli, the churchwarden of Seaton Ross, told me that he was very fond of Dad. He particularly enjoyed discussing and debating issues with Dad. Dave said that Dad was a towering intellect and very articulate. At the same time, Dave did comment to me that Dad sometimes expressed himself a bit like an express train who was so focused on what he was saying that he did not see when the train's carriages fell off the back. Dave talked to Dad about this, and Dave said that this helped Dad realise that people were not always ready for everything he wanted to express in the way he expressed it.

In terms of faith, Dave knew that Dad believed. When Dad took a service, he was not an entertainer with the congregation as the audience. For Dad, everyone was in church to worship God and the worship of God required the involvement of everyone there. Dave also commented that Dad was very much aware that all that was needed was to plant seeds in people's minds. Whilst Dave said that he did not know what impact Dad would have on someone, Dave felt that Dad did not need to know the impact he had. Dad was very aware that whatever resulted from the seeds planted, those results might not come to fruition until many years later and might not be attributed to him.

About 18 months before Dad died, Dad began to get increasingly tired. We did not know at this point that he had a serious heart condition. Dad asked Dave round for a coffee in order to talk to him about how the congregation could take part in the service. I realise in retrospect that Dad needed to find a way in which to keep celebrating the Eucharist in the way he was accustomed but with some assistance. Dave remembered that Dad spent several hours explaining the context and reasons for the help he was looking for. Dave found this explanation, which included a discussion of the relevant scriptures and the liturgy, amazingly useful.

Dave said that involving the congregation in Seaton Ross when Dad celebrated was a success. Dave had thought that many in the congregation would not have wanted to help because it was outside their comfort zone. However, whilst Dave was the main person who helped, others played their part. Dave felt that this was due to the fact that Dad made people feel comfortable and, probably more importantly, ensured that they knew exactly what they were doing and why.

Dad's ability to pull people together was a trait which Dianne Core from Londesborough really appreciated. Like Shelagh Jones, Dianne was very aware of the issues which existed in the parish of Londesborough. In fact, Dianne described the situation in Londesborough which Dad first stepped into as like coming into a disreputable family which is in bits and hurting. Dianne said that Dad managed to pull the congregation of Londesborough back together so that they were no longer fragmented. More than that, Dad got many of the people who had stopped coming back into church.

Dianne felt that Dad's peaceful presence was key to turning Londesborough around. Dianne said that Dad had a way of making people feel calm and reassured. Dad was able to see to the heart of someone's problems and help them to find a way through it. Even though Dianne did not wear her concerns about the Londesborough problems on her sleeve, Dad had the knack of knowing when something was eating at her and helped her deal with it.

Dianne summed Dad up as someone with compassion, respect and care for people and their needs. At the same time, she said that Dad was also not afraid to give someone a spiritual flea in the ear when he thought they needed it.

Dad made a great impression on all sorts of people regardless of whether they went to church or not. Paul Chielman is a Buddhist and was one of Dad's friends. Paul and Dad talked about many topics, but often of their own religious beliefs. For Paul, Dad was able to talk passionately about Christianity without being threatened by someone with different beliefs because Dad was so well versed in what he believed and the reasons why he believed it. Paul commented that many people say that they know about their religion, but few have the command of it as Dad had.

In order to make a great impression upon people you need to have a good memory and Dad certainly had that. I cannot recall how many times we would stop as I walked down the road with Dad. Dad would be saying hello to all sorts of people. When I asked Dad, "who was that?" the answer would be, I buried their mother or father, I married their son or daughter. Dad would remember both who they were and enough details about their family and circumstances to make that person feel special.

Sometimes you are remembered for the seemingly small things that you do, but which are significant for the person for whom you do them. After Dad had died, Mum was talking to Maggie Doyle, an old lady with dementia who lived in Londesborough. Despite her dementia, Maggie began telling Mum of how important Dad had been to her and her husband Patrick when Patrick was ill. Patrick had been brought up a Roman Catholic and had been taught Latin by the Jesuits. In later life he had lapsed, but would attend church with Maggie. I am not sure what was wrong with Patrick, but I understand that near to his death he was only able to communicate in Latin and not English. Dad visited Patrick regularly and spoke to Patrick in Latin. This and the fact that Dad had been able to administer the last rites to Patrick meant such a lot to Maggie.

Another example relates to the Turner family. Dad first met the family when he blessed the wedding of their daughter, Michelle. He would also take home communion to Peggy, Michelle's grandmother. A few years later, Michelle's father Mick became ill with a brain tumour. Dad heard about Mick's illness from a friend and began to visit him once a week. Mick was not a religious person, but he enjoyed Dad's company and visits. Sometimes they would talk, sometimes Dad would read to Mick, sometimes they would sit in silence. Mick's widow Sheila told me that Dad knew what to say to Mick to calm him down. Sheila said that it was as if Dad and Mick had known each other all their lives. As Andy, Mick and Sheila's son, said to me, the fact that they were not a religious family did not matter to Dad, Dad was just there to help.

During Dad's time in Market Weighton and the surrounding villages, he worked very closely with Nigel Strafford who was the then incumbent in the Holme-on-Spalding-Moor group of parishes which included Seaton Ross, Bursea, Bielby, Everingham and Harswell. Nigel recalls that as a colleague Dad was a "godsend". With so many small rural parishes, without Dad's help it would not have been possible to keep up the service rota that they did. Dad was ever-faithful and encouraging, doing whatever was asked of him. Just as importantly, Nigel says that Dad never "upstaged" him by courting his own popularity or by stirring up disloyalty.

At the same time, Nigel recalled that Dad certainly questioned what he saw as the lacklustre attitudes of some of the more recently ordained and their approach to the parochial life. Nigel felt that in this regard Dad may be seen as having a prophet-like role within his ministry. By that, Nigel said that Dad felt that it was important to speak out before values became so compromised that there was no way back. Dad believed firmly in the place, function, and role of the Church within God's Economy. When celebrating, Dad had a clear idea of the function of the priest. He valued order and having everything done properly. He detested sloppiness and things done half-heartedly.

As Nigel put it, "Dad's priesthood was essential to his own nature and his life with God, all mediated through the offices and discipline of the Church, her sacraments and her teaching".

Another of Dad's priest friends in Market Weighton was Peter Nelson. Peter and Dad met in 2009 when Peter retired as a hospital chaplain. Peter had originally been a Baptist minister but had become an Anglican priest. Over time. Peter had felt increasingly attracted to Anglo-Catholic spirituality and worship. Peter saw a kindred church spirit in Dad and he felt that together they flew the Anglo-Catholic flag.

Peter said that he particularly appreciated the straightforward and no-nonsense way in which Dad took a service. Dad would ring the bell and walk into church exactly on time. When he reached the altar, Dad would put on his spectacles and begin the prayers. There was no unnecessary chat or introduction.

Dad introduced the homily at the Market Weighton weekly Thursday morning Mass. Peter recognised that Dad did this because Dad saw the importance of teaching and explaining the faith. Peter said that he remembered, for example, a series of sermons which Dad preached on why candles and bells were used in church, why the priest wore the vestments and why it was important to genuflect. Dad preached these sermons because the congregation did not understand why these things were done.

As others have commented to me, Peter remarked that Dad had quite an imposing demeanor and seemed quite stern when you first met him. However, Peter said that as you got to know Dad you would see his sparkly personality and his wonderful smile. He recalled that Dad was not only a good raconteur of stories (especially ecclesiastical ones), but he was good at repartee, yet never in a hurtful or unkind way.

On 8th June 2013 Dad celebrated 50 years of ordination. He had wanted to celebrate a quiet Mass to mark the occasion. However, Mum, my sister and I wanted to do more for Dad so we invited as many people as we could who had known him over the years. It was a great testament to Dad that about 150 people came including his school friend John Bilton, his university friends Ian Donaldson and Geoffrey Steeley, a contingent from Adel (some of whom had been in Dad's Sunday school when he was a curate) as well as people from Market Weighton and the surrounding villages. Dad's anniversary was covered by the Pocklington Post, and he was even interviewed on Vixen FM, the local radio station.

True to form, Dad organised every aspect of the service with total precision. I remember being told by one of the priests involved that Dad had said that the procession from the vestry would commence at 11.29am exactly so that he would be standing at the high altar at 11.30am ready for the service to commence. Dad celebrated the Eucharist and Nigel Strafford preached the sermon. Dad wanted the sermon to be on the priesthood and not about himself. Nigel, of course, did slip in a mention or two of Dad in.

The service went wonderfully, and I remember that Dad gave quite an emotional speech during the buffet afterwards thanking everyone for coming, for the support that he had received from them and so many others during the course of his ministry and more than anything else for the love and unfailing help he had had from Mum.

Richard Seed, a former archdeacon of York was unable to be at Dad's service. However, the following email which he sent to Dad says it all.

"50 years is a wonderful achievement and I would like to congratulate you most sincerely. Your varied ministries in Adel, Hempton and Pudding Norton, Toftrees with Shereford, Pensthorpe, Colkirk and now around Market Weighton are all places I know will have and do now sincerely respect and admire your dedication, prayerfulness, pastoral sensitivity and above all your deep Love of God. Indeed any ministry not based on a love of and for God soon founders and yours has deepened over the years precisely because of your Love for Him who has called you to the Priesthood. So these 50 years could be truly summed up as REAL FAITHFULNESS – for which I and the Church remain deeply indebted. Many people over the years will have been touched in so many ways by your ministry and indeed some of them you may be even unaware of how you have helped them along the journey of life.

So congratulations on your splendid ministry. Congratulations on 50th years of Priesthood. Congratulations on your ongoing Vocation. Above all congratulations on your deep faithfulness to the God who has called you and whom you serve so loyally and prayerfully."

In April 2015, Dad celebrated his 80th birthday. As one of his presents Mum and I took him to Athens, where he had never been. It could only be Dad who at the top of the Acropolis would in one breath be talking about the ancient philosopher Socrates and in the next be pointing out the Ariopagus Hill on which St Paul preached to the Athenians (the sermon did not go down well, Dad said). I also remember Dad jumping on and off boulders and telling me with a twinkle in his eye not to tell Mum (who had stopped for a rest and was out of sight) since she would be cross with him.

Shortly after Dad's birthday Dad had a small heart attack and was told that he required bypass surgery. Although Dad's bypass surgery was a success, he developed kidney complications which resulted in his death on 10 December 2015. Despite Dad's ill health, he never lost his interest in the people around him. When he was in hospital having his bypass surgery the junior doctors would seek him out for a chat if they came onto the ward early. In fact, when Dad was later transferred to York Hospital certain of those junior doctors actually went to visit him when they had meetings in York. As Mum and Dad's GP said, Dad was a one off – junior doctors do not just chat to patients and they certainly do not visit them in other hospitals.

In the January after Dad had died, Mum was herself taken into hospital. One of the junior doctors who had treated Dad had been rotated onto Mum's ward. The doctor recognised Mum and asked her how Dad was. Mum said that he was quite distressed to learn that Dad had died. He told Mum that he thought that Dad was a wonderfully intelligent and interesting man who always had something to say and was so interested in the people that he met, despite the fact that he was seriously ill. I think that it is amazing that he not only remembered Dad but wanted to ask after him.

Dad commented on his 50th anniversary of ordination that God was "number one" in his life. But that did not mean that Mum or my sister and I ever felt that we were in second place. Since Dad's death, I have often wondered how Dad managed to square that seemingly impossible circle. Maybe Shelagh Jones was correct when she said that we, his family, enabled Dad to square the circle. We accepted Dad for who he was and supported him unquestioningly in his life and vocation.

What is a Christian?

We can all describe ourselves in many different ways. I can say that I am of average height, have green eyes and am cautiously outgoing. You may say that you are a tall, sporty beanpole who is something of a risk-taker. These statements immediately tell the listener something about a person's appearance and personality. I can also describe myself by saying, "I am a Christian". But what does it mean to say, "I am a Christian"? At its most basic it tells the listener that I am a follower of Jesus Christ. However, that statement in itself does not unpack the different characteristics of what it actually means to be a Christian, to live a Christian life. The thoughts in this chapter look at some of the key aspects of what it means to be a follower of Jesus Christ in practice.

The life of a Christian: come, do, go

Three commands of Jesus sum up or describe the life of the true Christian. The three commands are: come, do, go.

"Come", "come unto me", "follow me", is always Jesus' first call to us. Jesus doesn't begin by asking us to understand, or believe, or even repent. We have to do all those three things, but we can't do them if we aren't already answering Jesus' first call, "come unto me".

"Do this", the second command. "Do this", namely, what we should do each Sunday and as often as possible, the Lord's Supper, the Holy Communion, the Eucharist, the Mass, the Holy Mysteries. Call this service by whatever name we like; it expresses the fellowship between those who are responding to Jesus' first call: it also cements and strengthens the bond of fellowship.

"Go", "go into all the world", "go tell", is Jesus' invariable third order for all members of the Christian fellowship. The command Jesus lays upon all the members of his fellowship when we carry out his first two orders. "Coming to Christ" and "doing the Eucharist" helps us to acquire and absorb into ourselves the nature of Christ. The nature of Christ is the love of God. The love of God is utter and complete self-sacrifice and selflessness – God so loved the world that he gave his only begotten Son, and we must go tell the world that good news.

Several starting points focus our attention upon that three-fold rhythm of the Christian life. The Christian year, for example, tells the same story. In the course of the Christian year we follow the chief events in the life of Jesus and try to make them our own.

At the start of the Christian year Christmas and Epiphany centre around our singing "O come, let us adore him", getting to know him, to worship him, to understand the nature of his being and purpose.

Later on in the Christian year, Good Friday and Easter Day are the substance of which the service of Holy Communion is the shadow – who in the same night in which he was betrayed took bread and said: "*This is my body which is given for you*".[3] The Holy Communion is a memorial of Christ's death and passion, but not a memorial only, for Christ himself is present with us in this service in the power of his resurrected life and is binding us together in this great sacrament of unity.

Later on still, Ascension Day and Pentecost are the promise of Christ's presence with us always, the promise that he will strengthen and guide us when we carry on his work of making disciples from all nations – "*go therefore and make disciples of all nations...and remember, I am with you always, to the close of the age*."[4]

As well as the Christian year, the cross emphasises the three-fold rhythm of the Christian life. The cross is the symbol of the Christian faith throughout the world. Whenever we see it, it reminds us of our three

---

[3] Luke 22:19

[4] Matthew 28:19

Christian activities. Christ on the cross says to us, "Come unto me", "Draw closer", "Find your freedom in me", "Be crucified with me". The cross is the capital "I" crossed out, the symbol of self-sacrifice in the service of others, the only way to the good life.

Look at the cross again and see it as two arms joined to the centre. That way it reminds us of the body of Christ binding all his people into one fellowship, undivided like the shamrock, the clover, or the fleur-de-lys; the arms and body are all one person and we all grow up into the stature and fullness of him who fills all things.

We also see the cross as the plus or addition sign – the adding of more and more to the faith in proportion as we go forth from Calvary."*It is finished*"[5] – Christ's work is done, but only when he is lifted up will he be able to draw all men unto him: and that is our task on his behalf – "Lift high the cross, the love of Christ proclaim, till all the world adore his sacred name."[6]

The Christian year, the cross, and three abstract nouns sum up the true nature of the Christian faith. The three abstract nouns are Discipleship, Churchmanship and Mission. Those three words contain everything we need to learn about the Christian faith and practice. We cannot fully think of all three at one and the same time: yet it is impossible to divide the three – we cannot speak of any one of them to the exclusion of the others. Discipleship, learning more about Jesus, becoming an increasingly better friend of his, is possible only when it is based upon and lived in churchmanship.

Churchmanship itself is meaningless, certainly only a selfish pleasure, if it does not result in missionary endeavour. We can never speak of the Church without alluding or referring to both discipleship and missionary work – yet it's only as we realise more and more fully the

---

[5] John 19:30

[6] Words from the hymn by George William Kitchen

true meaning of the Church that we can really be disciples and missionaries.

To understand the Christian faith we have to approach it in several ways. Discipleship is our attempt to deepen our obedience to God, our attempt to extend our allegiance to Christ: the aim and object of our discipleship is personal holiness. Churchmanship, being lively members of the fellowship of the Church, is the realisation of our obligations and duties to each other. Our duty to God and our duty to our neighbour are strengthened and inspired by our duty to one another in the Church. Missionary work is the opportunity to test just how loyal we are to Christ as we sacrifice ourselves for others in telling them of Christ.

We must remember the three-fold rhythm of the true Christian life: Come – Do – Go. Discipleship, Churchmanship, Mission.

The Christian's individual relationship with God: personal salvation, fellowship, witness

I once had a friend[7] who was not only a priest: he was also a monk, a member of a Benedictine community[8] with its house in Buckinghamshire. My friend was well known as a spiritual director: many people went to him to make their confession and receive wise advice. He also was in great demand as a preacher, speaking effectively on many different occasions, whether it was the consecration of a bishop in St Paul's Cathedral in London or a Sunday morning service in a small village church somewhere in deepest Norfolk.

I always remember my friend saying to me one day, "You know, Stuart, priests usually have only one sermon in them, one over-riding message which they try to put across in different ways". I acknowledge that over the years I have "banged on", as it were, about the Christian's individual relationship with God. I have gone on and on about it in three

---

[7] Dom Robert Petitpierre

[8] The Anglican Benedictine community at Nashdom

different ways. I sum those ways up in these three phrases, "personal salvation", "community or fellowship" and "witness".

"Personal salvation". Actually, I'm not at all comfortable with that phrase. I come from a family that doesn't wear its heart on its sleeve; and I can't help casting my mind back to my college days[9] – earnest Christians in the college were in the habit of buttonholing people and asking, "Are you saved, brother?" I always wanted to quote to them the story about Professor Macaffy, one-time Provost of Trinity College, Dublin. Macaffy was asked one day if he had been saved – "Yes, indeed I have," he replied, "but it was such a narrow squeak I don't like to talk about it."

I have another reason for disliking the phrase, "personal salvation". Salvation is a technical term, and I try to avoid technical words if at all possible. Salvation is, of course, a convenient shorthand phrase for something that is vital and important: but too frequent use of the word "salvation" tends to make us think of a thing and not what is meant. To sum up – salvation refers, of course, to what Jesus did and accomplished for each one of us in being born into this world, living, dying, being raised from the dead, and going back to the Father. Salvation should always pose to us a question: are we truly alive to God, or are we dead to him, being over-whelmed by temptation and wrong-doing?

An old friend of mine was an ardent Pentecostal. She was always asking me if I was truly a born-again Christian. What she was saying our Anglican language sums up when it speaks of serving God not only with our lips but also in our lives. An old farmer I once knew gave a lovely illustration of the same point. He was complaining that the words of Church services were being changed, in particular the word "lively" was going to be dropped from the prayer for the Church. He remarked that he knew many people who were alive, but he was afraid that they were not at all lively.

---

[9] Dad was an undergraduate and scholar at Hertford College, Oxford between 1954 and 1958

The question is, therefore, "are we lively as a result of our faith?" God's word is lively but is he making us lively? Jesus came that we may have life and have it abundantly. If we Christians are not lively as a result of our faith, we shall never make the right sort of impact on all the non-Christian people around us. They will look at us and say, "What's the point of bothering about God when God seems to make little difference in their lives?"

Community or fellowship – I do not often meet former members of my old theological college in Salisbury nowadays, and, sadly, the college has been long closed down. When I do meet someone, however, we always mention Freddie Tindall, the Principal in our day. We used to call Freddie the "*koinonia* man". Freddie was an able and competent theologian, and full of insight into the ways of God with man. We called him "*koinonia* man" for good reason. He was always emphasising the importance of *koinonia*. Any discussion with him about college affairs, for example, whether the question at issue was how often there should be baked beans at breakfast or how a service in Chapel ought to be conducted, always led him to refer to the principle of *koinonia*. Not at all surprisingly really: after all, *koinonia* is one of the most important words in the Greek New Testament. *Koinonia* is the Greek word for fellowship or community: and no one can be a good Christian for very long if he or she is not an active and regular member of their local Christian community. The principles of Christian fellowship are the principles that ought to rule our lives.

Personal salvation and *koinonia* or fellowship leading to witness. I've always said that the true Christian is not only alive in Christ but lively in Christ. Moreover, the true Christian is never a solitary being but must be a regular and active member of the Christian community. It is only if we are regular and active members of the Christian community that we shall be good advocates for God. To be good advocates for God is a main reason for our existence.

The Christian is not just a moralist

What we say, and how we say it, is important. Not just the way we put our words together, though we have to be careful about that because we can end up saying something we didn't really intend. For example, a notice board outside a church once read: "The sermon this morning, "Jesus walks on water": the sermon tonight, "Searching for Jesus"."

If you don't like that example, what about this one? "At evening service tonight, the sermon topic will be, "Where's Hell?" Come early and listen to our choir practice."

Just as important is the tone of voice we use. The New Testament gives us a good example. A Pharisee was heard praying in the temple. He stood by himself and said, *"God, I thank you I'm not like other people: thieves, rogues, adulterers, or even like the tax-collector standing near to me. I fast twice a week: I give a tenth of all my income".*[10] Pride and self-congratulation dripped from the Pharisee's lips.

Very disturbing is a particular kind of Christian we can sometimes meet. The sort of Christian whose sole contribution to discussions on morals or how to behave, on the state of the nation and the contributions individuals may make to the national good, on the problems of having faith or a total lack of faith, is a proud and unhelpful, "Well, I'm a Christian", as though being a Christian in itself solved anything. It all depends on the sort of Christian we're claiming to be, since Christians can be rather like that Pharisee in the temple.

That's why the following words are so helpful. They came to me in a parish magazine sent to me every month. They're worth quoting:

When I say that I am a Christian
I am not shouting that I am clean
Living. I'm whispering, "I was lost,
But now I'm found and forgiven."

---

[10] Luke 18:9-14

When I say, "I am a Christian," I don't
Speak of this with pride. I'm
Confessing that I stumble and need Christ to be my guide.
When I say, "I'm a Christian", I am not
Trying to be strong. I am professing
That I am weak and need his strength to carry on.
When I say, "I am a Christian", I'm not
Bragging of success. I'm admitting that
I have failed and need God to clean my mess.
When I say, "I am a Christian", I am not
Claiming to be perfect. My flaws are
Far too visible but God believes I'm worth it.
When I say, "I am a Christian", I still
Feel the sting of pain. I have my share
Of heartache, as I call upon his name.
When I say, "I am a Christian", I am not
Holier than thou. I am just a simple
Sinner who received God's good grace somehow.[11]

These words are certainly worth thinking about and
pondering over: and if that's what we mean when we claim
to be Christians then there's hope for the world after all.

The Christian is a person to whom Our Lord Jesus Christ has entrusted other people

When I was a schoolboy, one of my heroes was Professor
Joad. If people remember Professor Joad today, they
remember him as an elderly academic who tried to get a free
ride on the railway by proffering an already used railway
ticket.

I remember Joad for something much more important,
however. In his hey-day Joad was often a panellist on the
1940s and 50s radio show, the Brains Trust. He used to help
the panel's discussions along by saying, "Well it all depends

---

[11] This appears to be a version of the poem, "When I say that I
am a Christian" by Carol Wimmer, published in 1992

on what you mean by…" whatever the topic was that was under discussion.

Whenever I hear the word "Christian" I want to do a Joad. The word "Christian" is used in so many different ways that it is almost meaningless. Perhaps most people use it in a moral sense. "It's not Christian", they say of something of which they disapprove. But how many moral or Christian pronouncements find universal approval? Even the commandment, "You shall not murder" has been questioned. Some versions, in fact, read differently. "You shall not kill", they say. There might seem to be little point to the difference; but the actual Hebrew word used originally really means, "You shall not kill unlawfully" – and that, of course, starts the huge debate of what is lawful and unlawful. I realised long ago that there is little agreement on what constitutes so-called Christian behaviour.

Perhaps we ought in future to use the word "Christian" only of someone who has been baptised? We can then check if a person is a Christian or not - we can look at the baptismal registers. That would allow us to say of someone that he or she is a good or bad Christian – do they come to the Holy Communion regularly and frequently, do they pray regularly and frequently, do they study the Bible regularly and frequently?

Another line of approach may be preferred. The two great commandments, that we are to love God and to love our neighbour, may give us an answer to the moral question of what it means to be a Christian. We can ask the question: what sort of behaviour is it that is to be expected of someone who is trying to love God and love their neighbour? Here something I read may help us towards a moral answer of what it means in general to be a good, baptised Christian. The Christian, I read, is a person to whom Our Lord Jesus Christ has entrusted other people.

Of course, two questions immediately occurred to me after reading that. Have all other people been entrusted to us? And, why and to what end have they been entrusted?

The first people to have a claim upon us are the members of our own families. They are literally the nearest, if not the dearest, ones God has given to us to care for and look after. Beyond the close circle of our relations there is the wider circle of friends and acquaintances. Providence has crossed their paths with ours for good or ill; it is our duty to see that it is always for good.

Then, there are the people we bump into or rub shoulders with as we go about our daily business. The story of the Good Samaritan[12] should be our guide here: we should not pass by anyone, wherever they are, whom we see to be in genuine trouble.

Finally, in today's global village we cannot escape being aware of the sorry plight of people in far distant lands. Up to now, humanitarian work has traditionally been carried out by such volunteer charities and agencies as Oxfam, Medicins Sans Frontieres, Save the Children, amongst others. Now, as war continues to be waged against the Taliban and ISIS, hard questions are being asked about world organisations: are the days of national security over? Has nationalism had its day? Nationalism is, after all, a comparatively recent affair, having emerged only after the 1789 French Revolution. Here appropriate questions may be: how many such wars on behalf of other people and for the sake of global security are both practical and affordable?

The second question, as to why other people have been entrusted to the Christian is perhaps easier to answer. God has entrusted them to us for the care and attention they need and such as we can provide. In this cruel and wicked world, we Christians are God's social workers: at our baptisms God appointed us as divine welfare agents to see to human needs.

The Christian has always done a great deal of hospital and medical work, much of it pioneering work; and that noble tradition must be continued. But one of the greatest troubles in the world today is the unfriendly and impersonal nature of contemporary society as currently organised – so

---

[12] Luke 10:25-37

many people feel lonely and lost, as if they are only a number on a form. That feeling leads to all kinds of problems, both mental and emotional as well as physical. That is why the care for which other people have been entrusted to the Christian is a care for the whole person – body, soul, mind and spirit.

One day John Baptist sent word to Jesus. He could not go to Jesus himself; he was in prison. He wanted to know who Jesus thought he was. Jesus made no direct answer; instead, he told John's messengers to report to John what they were hearing and seeing – *"the blind receive their sight,... the dead are raised up, and the poor have good news preached to them".*[13]

Even in his own day Jesus needed help in carrying out those good works. That is why he chose disciples and gave them their standing orders: cure the sick, raise the dead, cleanse the lepers, cast out demons.

Today's world population is, of course, much greater than it was in Jesus' day. Many more people are needing his care and his love today; and Jesus is now meeting their needs through the men and women he has called to be Christians.

St Teresa of Avila explained in a nutshell what we as Christians need to do in today's world:

"Jesus does not now stretch out of heaven his hands to heal; he puts them forth in ours. Ours are the eyes through which Christ now looks out in compassion on the world. Ours are the feet on which Jesus now goes about doing good. Ours are the hands with which Jesus now blesses. We then the baptised are Christ's body here on earth. Destroy all Church buildings throughout the world but the Church itself will continue forever, as long as Christian men and women continue Christ's caring work."

---

[13] Luke 7:22

Faith

St Matthew tells the story[14] of the man whose son is lying ill. This story is told also by St Luke in his gospel,[15] although in a slightly different version. There are also traces of the same story, with other slight differences, to be found in the gospel of St John.[16] Of the three versions of what seems to be the same story I prefer St Matthew's version for a variety of reasons which I will try to make clear as we have a closer look at St Matthew's version, with side glances at the other two.

The man whose son is lying ill is, in all three versions of the story, a Roman officer of the occupying power – Rome had turned Judea into a Roman province in around 6 A.D. The text calls this man a centurion, a commander of 80 men. St Luke makes him send some of the Jewish elders to Jesus with his request for help. For St Luke, the centurion is a person who thinks it best not to go to Jesus himself, but to send a delegation on his behalf. In St Matthew, however, the centurion approaches Jesus directly.

The centurion has a son. The actual Greek word used is ambiguous: it could mean either "son" or "servant", like our word "boy", which is the word the New English Bible uses. St Luke makes him a servant and has to explain his owner's action in sending for Jesus by adding the words "a favourite of his", otherwise the centurion would not have bothered about a mere servant. In St Matthew, however, there is no explanation of the man's actions because there is no need of one – we may take it that the boy is the man's own son, most dear to his heart, therefore.

The centurion walks straight up to Jesus and simply states the facts. My boy is lying at home paralysed and racked with pain. Jesus' reply is equally direct: I will come and cure him. But the officer is seized with compunction: "*Lord, I am not worthy to have you come under my roof?*" Neither Matthew

---

[14] Matthew 8:5-10

[15] Luke 7:1-10

[16] John 4:46-53

nor Luke gives the reason why the centurion said that. Was it because the Roman was aware of the prejudices of the occupied race? Jews never wanted to defile themselves by entering the home of a Gentile. Was it because he felt humble before the bearer of the almighty power to which he was making appeal?

Whatever the reason, the centurion's compunction is the occasion for still greater faith. There is, says the centurion, no need for Jesus to come in person: you need only say the word and the boy will be cured. For, the text goes on to say, "I am myself under orders" – that is certainly how we are to read St Luke's version of the story. We can get a meaning of a kind out of that reading, for we can say that Jesus was a man under the authority of his Heavenly Father just as the centurion was under the authority of his commanding officer.

But, unfortunately, that meaning of the phrase, "I am myself under orders" just will not do. For the words, "I myself", obviously mean that there is a parallel between the officer and Jesus, and the words which follow, "with soldiers under me. I say to one, "go", and he goes; to another, "come here", and he comes"; show where in fact the parallel between the centurion and Jesus lies. It lies in their both possessing the effective word of command. The original version must have read, therefore, "I also am a man in authority" – and there is some evidence to show that that is what St Matthew first wrote.

If St Matthew did write that, then we may begin to see the full force of what the centurion is saying. It is something like this. I know what it means for the battalion to freeze to attention at a single word from me. I in my sphere, you in yours, we both know from experience of the power of a word of command which is immediately obeyed. You need only say the word and my boy will be cured. The approach of the centurion draws astonishment from Jesus and high praise: "*I have not found such great faith, not even in Israel*".

But what is the basis of that superlative faith of the Roman officer? Its basis is not the Bible, it is not the Church, it is not even divine revelation, although it is worth noting that in St Luke's version of the story this is the basis of the centurion's faith. In St Luke's gospel the officer is on the edge of the Church, vouched for by the Jewish delegation as one who is a worthy man because he has built them a church.

Not so in Matthew's gospel, however. In St Matthew the basis of the centurion's faith is his natural life, his ordinary, workaday life, to the positive achievements of which, as well as to its limitations, he has paid due attention. For the centurion knows about soldiering: it is his job. He knows that there must be authority in this world, the authority of some men over others, if order is to be maintained, if chaos and evil are to be held in check, if peace of a kind is to be maintained.

That is a fact, a hard, inescapable fact for the centurion. All his energies and capacities as a soldier go into it. But is it just a fact and no more? If it is only a fact, then two courses lie open to the centurion. He must conclude either that life is simply a random collection of such facts without rhyme or reason, or else that he must try to extend that fact to cover everything else, and so try to make authority of that soldierly kind achieve more than it is really capable of, as if military tyranny *could* be the answer to the world's evil.

But what if it is not simply a fact? What if, when we try to look at life as a whole, such military authority is also a sign, a pointer, to what is like it and yet different, or to other kinds of authority extending even to the effective word of God himself? After all it was God who spoke and it was done, who said "*let there be light*"[17] and there was light? For there is an authority with a wider coverage than that of the soldier, which uses greater resources and penetrates further into the depths of life, and in Jesus the centurion recognises it: I am also a man in authority; you in your sphere, I in mine. In Jesus, the centurion recognises power of authority because he himself exercises a similar, albeit limited, power. But because Jesus is also the man of God and the man for

---

[17] Genesis 1.3

56

God, the centurion believes that he hears in Jesus' voice the final word of ultimate authority. In and through his own natural exercise of human authority the centurion has been led to acknowledge a heavenly and supreme authority which he believes he has heard from Jesus.

May I quote at length what one writer has said about faith in this context? "Faith is not a separable fragment of human behaviour, nor is unbelief a detachable thing done in the midst of other things. Faith is not a wish that remains unfulfilled, nor is unbelief the refusal to stretch out towards some distant goal. To believe is to apprehend human action, all human action, in its relation to God: not to believe is not to recognise the only context in which human behaviour can be anything but trivial. The man who believes apprehends that every visible human act requires to be fulfilled by the invisible, corresponding, and creative action of God. The man who believes recognises that all human behaviour is by itself and in itself incomplete. The man who believes knows that God fills up this incompleteness, and that, in filling it up, he makes of the human act a thing that has been wrought in God. But the generality of men hate that exposure of their behaviour. They will not face the pain of it. They do not think that their actions required to be fulfilled. Or, if they do recognise their own inadequacy, they do not believe in the possibility of their behaviour being made good. These men are atheists."

What shall we do then with our lives, our natural, pagan lives, our ordinary, workaday lives? Shall we see in them an all-sufficiency that will give us the final satisfaction here on earth? Or shall we see in them signs and pointers to that alone which can fulfil them? Take, for example, medicine – a good work indeed; but what lasting profit is it to prop up the sick for a few years and restore them to a world where death is the final truth? Or take the force and the majesty of the law, without which evil goes unchecked and the weak are the victims of the strong; but which, nevertheless, is powerless to secure glad obedience to that law of good which God writes in the heart. There are also politics and social service, necessary facts of life if ever there were any, since people are made to live in society; but do politics and social service, can politics and social service, for all their contriving, build that city which has firm foundations because its architect and builder is God? There are teaching and learning without which we are brutes; do they give us the final answer? Or are they but broken and fitful lights of the radiance of that wisdom in which we know as we are known?

Or shall we, one day then, as the best way of all, move in and through our natural lives towards their supernatural fulfilment? And shall we do so through the Christ in whose human life we see the showing forth of the supernatural? Shall our ordinary everyday lives become the raw material of our faith, the jumping-off ground towards perfection? Or are Church people to be simply spoilt pagan people whose natural lives are ruined, made worse than they would ordinarily have been, since they became members of the Church? Or may we see in Church people that enriching of ordinary human life which comes about through commitment to the cause of Christ? Church people everywhere, are your lives being enriched and transformed through your belief in the Christ as you move towards your supernatural fulfilment along the lines of what is good in your natural lives?

The job of the Christian

St John's gospel is at once the easiest and the most difficult gospel to read. The text, "*I chose you out of the world*"[18], shows that. Seven short words, so short that we read them almost without thinking. Yet they are the best description of the Christian job in life that we have ever been given.

"*I chose you.*" We know, in theory, that God is at the back of everything, that he is the maker of heaven and earth. But we tend to think that he made heaven and earth once, long

---

[18] John 15:19

ago, and that now they are turning over under their own steam. Yet, "maker" is present tense. God is making heaven and earth all the time, continually keeping them in being by his inexhaustible energy, continually replacing old and worn out parts. We acknowledge that fact in the general Thanksgiving when we thank him for our creation and preservation, when we thank him for having made us out of nothing and, having made us, for keeping us alive. If we look into the matter carefully, we shall find that our only and never-ending support in life is our Heavenly Father.

In the same way, God has chosen us out of the world. He chose us once, long ago. To be strictly correct, we should say that he chose us before the world began – for his plans are everlasting – but he had to wait for us to be born before he could tell us of his plans. Once we were born, however, he was able to tell us of his choice and tell us in his own good time, when the time was right, when there was every chance we could agree to having been chosen – for we cannot choose to be chosen. Choosing us out of the world is our Father's prerogative. We cannot demand it from him as of right. We can only give thanks for it once he has done it. As in everything else, we have to await his pleasure.

Now, just as we forget that God is continually making heaven and earth, continuously keeping all things in existence by his almighty power, so we forget that having chosen us out of the world he goes on choosing us, chooses us afresh at the start of every new day. For one day is never like another. Each day brings with it an unknown set of circumstances in and through which we have to catch the sound of our Father's voice and learn what it is he is wanting us to do during the next 24 hours. He chose us out of the world, and he goes on choosing us, and we have continually to respond if we don't want to fall back into the world.

The world out of which we have been chosen cannot be summed up in a word. Briefly, it is the situation of everything that has been organised contrary to our Father's will and plans. The world of the sleazy night clubs and drugs barons, the world of big business and the takeover bid, the world of binge drinking and casinos. In short, all the ways in which we offend our Father in heaven by misusing the good things he has given us. But, blessed be the Lord our God, for he has chosen us out of that world and put us into the life of heaven which we are enjoying here and now.

The line used to be taken by preachers of old that what they had to do was to persuade people away from the fires of hell and into the delights of heaven. But the New Testament teaches us that our Heavenly Father has already given us the pleasures of heaven. Here and now, by virtue of our baptism we are, to a greater or lesser extent, already living the heavenly life. With a tender and loving hand, our Father washed us clean in baptism and gave us the power to enter paradise. No one can take that privilege away from us although we can lose it by refusing to join in the life of heaven and falling back into the world.

The other side to our text are the words, "I send you". If our Father has chosen us out of the world it was for a purpose that he did so. And the words, "I am sent", are the words our Lord uses to describe himself more than any other, so that we should be proud to know that he is sending us even as he was sent. Of course, our hearts may fail us when we remember what his being sent resulted in, and we fear that the same may happen to us. Many of us would probably fall by the wayside instantly if we had to suffer only a fraction of what our Lord had to suffer.

But really, there is no cause for too much alarm. We must recognise that dangers will face us - our Lord never lets his friends walk into things with their eyes closed, "*if you were of the world the world would love you as its own; but you are not of the world... therefore world hates you*".[19] The great comfort is that our Lord is in charge. Just as we could not even ask to be chosen but could only await his pleasure, so we know that he is sending us into the world in the name and power of his Father who is now our Father. We are not going it alone, sent from a remote HQ into an area in which

---

[19] John 15:19

we have no lines of communication with base; "*I am with you always, even unto the end of the world.*"[20]

If that were not so, if Christ were not with us always, we could have no hope of succeeding in our mission, which is to turn the world back into the right direction, to turn it towards God. For our job in life as Christians is to be hinges, the hinges on which the world moves to face the Father. We are the intermediaries between the Father and the rest of the world, the means, the instruments he uses to bring the world to perfection. We must therefore accept our mission and bend our will to our sender's, only so will we begin to achieve results.

The fact that our baptism has already put us into the life of heaven is the best, the only, way to fulfil our mission. As more and more we live out the heavenly life here on earth, the more successful we become as representatives of heaven. It is as if we can think of the life of the world as a horizontal line; and the life of heaven as a vertical line. The more representatives of heaven there are, therefore, the better representatives we become, the stronger will become the vertical line as it strikes the horizontal, the more chance heaven will have of coming down and spreading out along the horizontal line until the whole earth is lifted up into heaven itself.

"*I chose you out of the world*". That is the Christian life in a nutshell, and there incidentally, is the biggest argument for the Church, because it is only in and through the Church that the two worlds of heaven and earth can meet. An individual is not a Christian, therefore, who is not a member of the Church. An individual is a bad Christian who does not worship in Church, and if an individual is a bad Christian that individual is a weak point in the vertical line by which heaven and earth become one.

---

[20] Matthew 28:20

Christians from across the ages help us to live the Christian life

Some people think that the worship of the Church is dull and boring. They think that to live the Christian life is dreary and irksome. No doubt, we have all felt the same at one time or another. And there is no reason why we should not have felt like that. If anybody tells you that the Christian life is easy you can be sure of one thing, that person has not even begun to live the Christian life. But although the Christian way of life is not easy, we shall always find help along the way if we look for it, and there are many directions in which we may look for help. Chief of all the ways is to turn our eyes in the direction of God, for he alone is our sure and certain help. But there are other ways in which we may find help on the Christian road, ways provided for us by God himself, ways to be used in addition to the way of looking towards God.

One of those other ways is to find help from other members of the Church. I do not mean from the members of the Church who are on earth. Perhaps you do not like your fellow Christians. Perhaps their very appearance, or the sort of people they are, puts you against them. If so, you are hardly likely to be helped by them, unless you look more deeply into them and see them as they really are, like yourself, a child of God, loved by God and of unique importance to him. So, when you find yourself put off by your fellow Christians, stop yourself for a moment and look at them properly. I sometimes think that being a Christian is like wearing a pair of bifocal spectacles. You look at your fellows through the top half of your spectacles and you see nothing out of the ordinarily about them, but look at them more closely, through the bottom half, and you may see them as they really are, creatures of God.

But a more certain way of finding help from other members of the Church is to look at those of them who are no longer on earth. Look at some of the Christian men and women who lived in the past – they are still alive in the communion of saints – and see what help you may receive from them. As an example of what I mean, let us have a close look at St James, apostle and martyr, whose feast day we celebrate on 25 July.

First, we need to remember an incident which took place in Galilee. The three special friends of Jesus (James, together with his brother, John, and Peter) had had the privilege of being alone in the hills with Jesus and of seeing suddenly something of Jesus' glory – while Jesus was praying the appearance of his face changed and his clothes became dazzling white, and out of the cloud there came a voice: "*this is my Son, my Chosen one; listen to Him*".[21] After that episode those three disciples were more certain than ever that Jesus was the Son of Man and they knew also that they themselves were to some extent involved in his work, and a separate class from the rest of mankind.

Imagine the surprise of those disciples, therefore, at what happened immediately after their return from the hills. They have been told that they were to follow Jesus but when they tried to imitate him and to cast the devil out of a child they could not do so. And the failure was made public. The boy's father shouted out in front of everybody else exactly what had happened: "*I begged your disciples to cast the devil out but they could not.*"[22] And in front of everybody else Jesus rebuked them for their lack of trust in him. It was a hard lesson in humility for the disciples, a lesson of dependence. They had to be taught that their special relationship to Jesus did not give them any powers of their own – they had to learn that they were always and completely dependent upon him.

That was not the only lesson in humility which the disciples had to learn. Master, said John, voicing what was also in the mind of his brother James, we saw a man casting out devils in your name, but as he is not one of us, we tried to stop him. Jesus said to him, do not stop him, for he who

---

[21] Luke 9:35
[22] Luke 9:40

is not against you is on your side.[23] That was the disciples' second lesson in humility. It was true that they had been called by Jesus and that they had accepted his call and that they were therefore to some extent in the class by themselves. But that did not mean that they were the only people who were doing God's work. The disciples had to realise that there were others besides themselves who were being faithful to God in the way to which he had called them, like the exorcist whose name we do not know. This is also a lesson to apply to ourselves. We should not pride ourselves upon our membership of the Church and think that ours is the only one way to heaven. It is only the way which God has given to us, and we should not think that he prevents others from following different ways to him. Other sheep which are not of this fold are many and who are also at present outside the Church but may enter into the kingdom of heaven before many Church people.

On another occasion James and his brother cried out together at what they thought was an intolerable rudeness to Jesus. The episode goes like this. As the time approached when Jesus was to be taken up to heaven, he set his face resolutely towards Jerusalem, and sent messengers ahead. They set out and went into the Samaritan village to make arrangements for him; but the villagers would not have him because he was making for Jerusalem. When the disciples James and John saw what had happened, they cried out, Lord, may we call on fire from heaven to burn them up? But Jesus turned and rebuked them, and they went on to another village.[24]

What other great lesson that was for James to learn. You cannot bully or force people into accepting Jesus. If they do not welcome him into their lives on the first occasion of his asking for entry, he does not want to leave them in such a state that they will never again have the opportunity to accept him, as the villagers would have been left. Jesus is

---

23 Luke 9:49-50, Mark 9:38-39

24 Luke 9:53-55

not like us. If we offer our love and it is spurned, we are rarely willing to offer it again. But Jesus is always knocking at the door of a person's heart, insistently knocking but how gently, for he respects a person's privacy. That is why I so much dislike the hot gospelling methods of evangelism with their strident cry of "come forward now", "now is the time". We should be as gentle with other people in bringing them to God as Jesus was.

James and his brother John must often have exasperated their fellow disciples, and most of all perhaps when they asked Jesus to do them a favour. "*Master, we would like you to do us a favour.*" "*What is it you want me to do?*" he asked. They answered. "*Grant us to sit in state with you*".[25] The other disciples were, of course, indignant with James and John when they heard what they had asked. But before becoming indignant they would have done well if they had thought a little more carefully about that conversation which James and John had had with Jesus. For after Jesus had told them that they did not understand what they were asking for he asked them a question – "*can you drink the cup I drink, or be baptised with the baptism with which I am to be baptised*".[26] Of course, neither James nor John understood what Jesus was asking them. They did not know what he was going to suffer though they suspected from his manner that something dreadful was about to take place. And yet, such was their loyalty to Jesus, their blind loyalty, they said that they could. Now, the world despises such loyalty and I think that each one of us must confess that we are afraid to give such loyalty, for there is no telling where such loyalty will lead us – it led St James to lose his head, the first of the 12 apostles to suffer martyrdom. But blind loyalty is what Jesus asks of each one of us. We have to give ourselves to him without reserve, unconditional surrender, no saying to ourselves, well, if things become too bad on the Christian

---

[25] Mark 10:37

[26] Mark 10:38

way I can always pull out; such half-hearted devotion is no good to Jesus – he wants our all.

St James, apostle and martyr, whose feast day we celebrate on the 25th day of July every year. Whenever you are tempted to think that you are sure to enter the kingdom of heaven because you are a member of the Church, remember the unknown exorcist who cast out devils in Jesus' name but who was not one of the official 12 and realise that there are people who are not members of the Church who are doing God's will and – maybe – doing it better than you. Secondly, never try to use force upon people when you are trying to persuade them to accept Jesus, as James and John allowed themselves to become bitter against the Samaritans who refused Jesus. Follow the example of Jesus and lead them into holiness. Thirdly, give yourself entirely to Jesus, not keeping anything back, even though you cannot know beforehand what will happen to you after you have given yourself to him. When the Christian way seems long and dreary, hard and irksome, see St James in the glory of paradise and in seeing that glory you will be helped along your way.

The Christian life is one of joy

The New Testament is the book of joy. In it the words "to rejoice" occur 72 times, and the word "joy" occurs 76 times. Throughout, on almost its every page, we hear the note of joy. When the angel came to Mary to tell her of the child she was to bear, his greeting was, "Rejoice," or "Joy be with you". On the Resurrection morning the greeting of the Risen Christ to men who had come to mourn was, "Joy be with you".

The Church decided at the Council of Jerusalem[27] to open its doors to the Gentiles and its leaders sent a letter to the Gentiles informing them of the decision, the letter began, "Joy be with you". St James wrote a general letter to the Christians scattered throughout the world, and his first

---

[27] The Council of Jerusalem occurred in around 50A.D.

words were, "Joy be with you". Almost the last words that St Paul wrote to his friends at Corinth were, "Joy be with you". The greeting, "Joy be with you", rings triumphantly throughout the pages of the New Testament.

It would be strange if the New Testament were not the book of joy because joy is one of the marks of the Christian life. Whatever else we might say about it – and we can say a great deal – the Christian life is a life of joy. The kingdom of heaven, wrote St Paul to Romans, is the kingdom of righteousness and peace and joy; therefore, just as we have a taste of the kingdom of heaven here on earth, so already we know its joy.[28] *"Rejoice in the Lord"*,[29] Paul went on to say to his Philippian friends, a command he repeated to the Thessalonians[30], while for the Colossians he prayed that they may be strengthened with all power, according to God's glorious might, for all the endurance and patience, with joy.[31] It has been well said, therefore, that "Rejoice" is a standing order for the Christian.

The New Testament tells us of certain areas of life in which the Christian may be sure of joy. There is, for example, the joy of Christian fellowship, the joy of what we might describe as "togetherness". It is a joy even to see and experience such fellowship. It is a joy to see such fellowship restored after it has been broken. It is also a joy to see Christian fellowship reunited. The New Testament knows nothing of a religion which isolates us from our fellow Christians. The New Testament knows vividly the joy of making friends, keeping friends, and of friends being reunited. It could not be otherwise, for friendship between two people is a reflection of the friendship between God and man.

There is also the joy of the gospel, the joy of the new discovery made known to us. It was tidings of great joy that

---

[28] Romans 14:17

[29] Philipians 4:4

[30] Thessalonians 5:16

[31] Colossians 1:11

the angels brought to the shepherds in the field by night, and the wise men rejoiced when they saw the star which told them of the birth of the King. So, in the beginning there was joy. There was also joy at the very end when, according to St Luke's account of the matter, the disciples returned to Jerusalem after the Ascension with great joy.[32] The gospel-story, therefore, begins and ends with joy. It was with joy that Zacchaeus received our Lord into his house. The Thessalonians heard about the Lord with joy. Time after time Acts of the Apostles tells of the joy which came to people when the gospel arrived among them. The New Testament makes it clear that the gospel is the occasion for joy.

We hear so much about joy in the New Testament, but it is notable how often joy and affliction walk hand in hand. Christian joy is perhaps like the joy of a woman whose labour has passed and whose child has come. Likewise, St James bids his readers to count it all joy when testing comes,[33] and indeed in spite of persecution the Christians in Antioch were filled with the Holy Spirit and with joy. Perhaps, however, the most startling passage in the whole of the New Testament is when St Paul says that he rejoices in his suffering. *"In my flesh,"* he says, *"I am filling up what is lacking in Christ's afflictions."*[34] It is difficult, however, to see how that can be so. I always find the following illustration will be of help.

In his laboratory or operating theatre or research room a scientist or a surgeon or a physician toils and sweats and labours and suffers and endangers and risks his or her own health to find some cure or some help for the pains and ills of others. But that discovery remains useless until it is taken out of the laboratory and made available all over the world. And it may well be that those who take it out have to sweat and toil and suffer and sacrifice to make it available. So that

---

[32] Luke 14:52
[33] James 1:2
[34] Colossians 1:24

we may say that their sufferings to make the gift freely available fill up and complete the sufferings of the great man or woman who made the original discovery.

Now, the work of Jesus Christ is done and completed. But it has still to be made known to mankind. Time and time again in history people have laboured and suffered and died to tell others of that which Jesus Christ did for them. And in their sufferings, they may well be said to be completing the sufferings of Jesus Christ himself. There, then, is the great uplifting thought, there is the note of joy, that if ever our loyalty to Jesus and our service of him cost something, it means that we too are completing the sufferings of Jesus Christ. There can be no higher privilege than that since that is so, then it is true that ours is a joy which no one can take from us.

The world we live in seems to be on a knife's edge. We live in challenging and difficult times. To put it in Biblical terms, the evil one is walking the earth and the days of war have been unleashed yet again. But we have an everlasting joy, Jesus Christ, our Saviour. The elements may beat against us, earth, fire, air, and water: the power of evil may penetrate into our innermost heart, but if we stand firm in the power of our Lord, we shall always rejoice. Know the joy of the gospel.

Christian love

You will not be surprised to learn that I love my wife and our two daughters. I also loved the cocker spaniel dog given to me when I was 11 years old. I hope you will not disapprove of the fact that I love a gin and tonic before dinner. You may be amused too that I love a rich and scrumptious dessert called, "Mrs Langan's chocolate pudding" – whipped cream wrapped around with a rich covering made from cocoa and chocolate.

The word "love" is one of the most overworked words in the English language. We use it to cover many different situations: the love between a husband and wife, love of animals, parental love, love for the good things of this life.

When a Gaelic-speaking lad loves a Gaelic-speaking lass there are, I am told, more than 20 different ways for him to tell her so. The poor English lad who loves an English lass has to make do with one word, "love".

When Jesus was alive the then civilised world used Greek as its common language. That common Greek language had several words for love:

There was, first of all, *eros*. Think of the statue of Eros – that famous little statute in Piccadilly Circus in London; and you will realise that *eros* is the Greek word for physical or sexual love.

Then the Greeks used the word *philia*. We use that word in English, for example philosophy, which means love of wisdom or knowledge. *Philia* was, perhaps, the highest word the Greeks had for love. *Philia* referred to a warm, intimate, tender relationship, involving body, mind and soul. That is why paedophiles should be referred to more accurately as pederasts.

Philia may have been the Greek word for a noble kind of love or relationship. There was, however, something missing from that relationship. Shakespeare expressed it very well when he said in sonnet 116, "love is not love which alters when alteration finds" and the Book of Common Prayer emphasises that fact in the marriage service when it speaks of love being "for better, for worse, for richer, for poorer, in sickness and in health".

Even earlier than the Book of Common Prayer and Shakespeare, the ancient Greek philosopher Aristotle had pointed out a great defect in the general idea of love. Aristotle pointed out that the "lover's pleasure is gazing at his beloved, the loved one's pleasure is in receiving the attentions of her lover, but when the loved one's beauty fades, the friendship fades too, as the lover no longer finds pleasure in the sight of his beloved, and the loved one receives no attention from the lover".

Philia may have been the noblest kind of love the ancient world knew but there was nothing in the ancient world to preserve the warmth of love when attraction grew old.

70

The New Testament uses an entirely new word for love, a word that with its New Testament meaning had not been used before. That should not surprise us: the New Testament has an entirely new kind of love to speak of; a type of love never met with before. That word is *agape* – *agape* is a new word for a new love, a love that would have been thought impossible until Our Lord Jesus Christ came and showed it to us.

Archbishop Trench[35], of Ireland, was one of the first people to make a detailed study of the use of words. Here is what he said about *agape*.

"*Agape* is a word born within the bosom of revealed religion. *Agape* is a new word to express a new attitude towards other people, an attitude born within the Christian fellowship and impossible outside the Christian fellowship."

Christianity is a fine and noble religion and, thanks be to God, it is a very practical religion. Christianity not only lays before us the highest ideal: it also shows us how to attain that ideal. Our Lord Jesus Christ, the human face of God, is the practical demonstration of the new kind of love. Jesus gave us the best object lesson in how to love. He summed up that lesson by telling us to love "*as I have loved you*".[36]

Jesus loved his disciples. The disciples were by no means perfect. They had many failures and shortcomings; but Jesus loved them and wanted the best for them. To that end Jesus gave, gave himself, totally unreservedly, without holding anything back. Finally on Calvary's hill he gave up everything he was. Calvary is important because first and foremost it expresses just how much Jesus loves us. Jesus is the living example of *agape*, the new kind of love.

Agape, therefore, is unconquerable benevolence. *Agape* is indefatigable, invincible goodwill. *Agape* always wants the highest good for other people. *Agape* involves the whole of our personalities, it is not a matter of our feelings and

---

[35] Richard Trench (9 September 1807 – 28 March 1886) became the Anglican Archbishop of Dublin in January 1864.

[36] John 13:34

emotions only, it is a matter of our minds and our wills also. The following words I read somewhere may serve as a short but good description of *agape* – "love is not measured by the beating of a heart but by the actions of the hands". However unlovable, however unlikeable others may be, we have to love them, try to do what is best for them, want only what is best for them – love them, as Jesus loves us.

A once popular song referred to the "love that makes the world go round". *Agape*, Christian love, loving others as Christ loved us, is the only love that really makes the world a better place. *"Love, one another"* said Our Lord Jesus Christ, *"as I have loved you"*[37] – and however unattractive and unlovable we are, Jesus loves us to the end; and the end for Jesus was death on Calvary's cross. Every time we fail to love we are driving yet more nails through Jesus' hands on the Cross.

The Church is part of the world

One wonders what the future holds for our parish churches. Two comments often made about the Church should perhaps guide our thinking. The first comment; "it does you good to get away from it all and come to church". The second comment; "you can't expect people to come to church when what goes on inside church seems to have no bearing on the rest of the world". A churchgoer made the first comment; a non-churchgoer the second. Both comments reveal the same ignorance about Jesus.

Acts of the Apostles tells us that Jesus is Lord of all, but people don't think of Jesus as Lord of all. They think of him only as Lord of the Church, Lord of a select group of people, exclusive, separated from the world and its concerns. For many people Jesus seems to live in the Church, from which he sends his disciples to make contact with life outside. Such people see the Church's task as one of communication with those outside the Church, a reaching out to establish contact with non-Church members. They think of the Church as

---

[37] John 13:34

having to learn the language of the world outside, as though they are strangers to it – "the great problem of today", a church leader once said, "is to build a bridge between Sunday and Monday".

What a wrong idea about the Church that church leader had. Jesus is Lord of all, not just Lord of the Church. God created the universe, the whole world. Genesis[38] tells how God began, not with the Sabbath, the holy day, but with the first day of the working week. It was on that first day of the week that God created light, a main requirement for the life that goes on day by day in the home, the office, the factory, and the shop. God's work, through Jesus, as described in the New Testament, is the renewal and restoration of the whole world. We must remember that God loved the world so much that he sent his Son to give it the possibility of new life, eternal life, the best life there is. Jesus is Lord of all, now, not at some future time when the world will somehow have been turned into the Church.

Christians themselves can cause Jesus to be thought of as Lord of the Church only, and not as Lord of all the world. For Christians sometimes treat the Church as a stained-glass window world, divorced from, cut off from, the hard facts of the real world outside. That view of the Church isn't true to the central events of the Christian good news. Those central events took place in the world. Their main figure wasn't a member of the clergy, but a lay-man, a carpenter and a working man, the sort of man you would send for to do your roof. The events occurred in a city, the sort of place featuring in any day's headlines. Church people were conspicuous by their absence from the scene. It wasn't a Church person who carried Jesus' cross for him on the way to Calvary but an African Jew. Jesus promised paradise not to a Church person but to a condemned criminal. Every time they come to church Christian people say the creed but the first person to recite the credal profession that Jesus is the Son of God was a pagan, an officer in the army of occupation

---

[38] Genesis 1:5

on the Jewish territory. The first witnesses to Jesus' triumph over death weren't Church leaders but people on the fringe, the women intent on attending his corpse. Two of the people to whom the risen Jesus appeared and whom he commissioned as his principal witnesses were Peter, an apostate disciple who had denied him with curses, and Paul a leading persecutor of the Church.

The central events of the Christian good news took place in the world, in the equivalent of a Monday setting, before and after the holy day of the Sabbath. That's why the good news is news for the whole world because it concerns the whole world – it is not confined to that tiny part of the world that finds itself in church. In the gospel God isn't beginning to create a new world. He is claiming the existing world as his own, renewing and cleansing it – the whole world, with its everyday life of business and industry and personal relationships, the whole world is God's prime concern.

The Church is better described as that part of the world which has already accepted the message intended for everyone. The Church is simply that part of God's creation which already knows that everyone stands under God's judgement and forgiveness. The Church is just that group of people who already acknowledge that everyone is called to praise and worship God as creator. The Church witnesses to Jesus not as Lord of itself but as Lord of all. The Church doesn't have to approach the world from outside as it were; it doesn't have to try to establish contact with those outside as though they were strangers.

The Church witnesses to Jesus within the world, as itself part of the world and from within the Monday situation. The Church exists for the sake of the world of everyday life. Jesus is Lord of all; and the Christian's truest place of service, the altar of his greatest sacrifice, is in the weekday world, the daily life of work and personal relationships in which we are called to die daily and daily rise to new life. The command to love our neighbour as ourselves isn't the same as the command to love the Lord our God. The command to love our neighbour is the chief way in which we express our love of God. When we love our neighbour as ourselves, we are indeed acknowledging Jesus as Lord of all. For then, and then only, are we living as God would have all people live. And when we are doing that, we aren't getting away from it all and coming to church; we are not building a bridge between Sunday and Monday – we are starting where God started, with the work-a-day world and bringing it all with us as we come to church. It is for the sake of all the parishioners of each parish church, whether they come to church or not, and for the whole of their daily living, that each parish church exists. Each parish church is both a symbol and agent of Jesus, Lord of all.

Questions for discussion or reflection

- *What do you mean when you say, "I am a Christian"?*
- *Thinking about the points made in the thoughts in this chapter:*
  - *which points most chime with your own personal experience and why?*
  - *did any of the points made surprise you and, if so, why?*
- *What change(s) (however small or large) should you make to your life to make it a more fully Christian one? How easy or difficult is it to do this? What steps are you able to make to try to achieve this?*

Prayer and the Bible

In today's world we are spoilt for choice when it comes to the different ways in which we can communicate with each other. We can speak face to face, on the telephone or over the internet. We can send emails and text messages. We can use any number of Apps and social media platforms. However, in our busy and fraught lives it can be all too easy to lose touch with friends and to fail to communicate often and meaningfully with loved ones. Prayer is the way in which we communicate with God. Just as there is no one size fits all way in which we should communicate with each other, there is no one size fits all way to pray. This chapter looks at some of dos and don'ts of praying and suggests some prayer techniques. The chapter also reminds us of the importance of the Bible reading and Bible study.

What is prayer?

It is good to ask ourselves from time to time how we are to pray. Books and books and books have been written about prayer, how to pray and how not to pray. I would like to put forward only a few points about saying our prayers.

First of all, the word prayer itself. What does it mean? We all know what it's like to say prayers. The dictionary meaning of the word tells us that prayer means asking for something. And perhaps that is what most of us mostly do in the majority of our prayers. Even in the Lord's prayer... give us this day our daily bread, forgive us our trespasses, lead us not into temptation... And what's more, probably most of the prayers we make up for ourselves are nothing but asking for something, asking, asking, asking. I sometimes ask myself if God finds all that asking that we do very boring. Rather like listening to somebody talking about themselves the whole time.

Of course, the Bible tells us that if we ask it will be given to us, for everyone who asks receives. Just as children very often want chocolates or large pieces of cake. I may be somewhat old fashioned but even in today's more relaxed society I think that before they are given the chocolates or cake, children should have to say "please, may I?" In my house at least, if they don't remember their manners, they are not likely to be given what they want. Maybe sometimes we try to bully God, presenting him with a list of what we would like done just as if he were a junior work colleague.

And another point about all that asking we do of God. We sometimes have to say to people, after we have known them for a time, oh dear, he or she is becoming big headed, taking everything for granted, never bothering to say thank you when you've done something for him or her. We all know such people. Perhaps if we admit it, we all have something of such people in ourselves. And never more so perhaps than in our dealings with God. I am sure that we do not say thank you to God half enough. We are too busy telling him what we want next even when he's just given us something.

Now when we go to the supermarket and look for something, if it is not in stock, we usually make do with something else. But if we wanted something very much and it isn't in stock, we are inclined to grumble that it is not available, saying that the supermarket's not very efficient and we look to see whether or not we can get the item online. What is our reaction, then, when we do not get what we want from God? There is the possibility that we may have asked him for the wrong thing, for something God couldn't possibly give us, not because he hasn't got the power but because it would be out of character for him to do so.

Sometimes, however, it is not a matter of our not being given what we have asked for. We just do not seem to be given any answer at all. That's a difficult problem. What do we do in such a case? I'm reminded of the story of the little girl who wanted an expensive doll for Christmas which her parents could not afford. Long before Christmas the little girl began to ask for her doll. Christmas came and went, and no doll appeared. The little girl's mother was quite worried. She wondered what the effect on her daughter would be, that

God had made no answer to her prayer. So, one day she asked her, "Darling, were you terribly disappointed that God didn't answer your prayer about the doll?" The mother was surprised when her little daughter turned to her and said indignantly, "Mummy, he did – he said no."

Prayers. Saying prayers. Perhaps the best description of our prayers is that they are talking with God as one friend to another. But God is more than a friend can ever be to us. Without God we are nothing. We depend entirely upon him. There is a mistake we sometimes make. We do not behave as though we do depend on God. All we do is look at ourselves, think about ourselves, so that our prayers are full of ourselves, not of God.

There is one simple but effective way to remember how we should pray. Let's picture to ourselves the garden, the garden of Gethsemane. Only four people are in the garden, and one of them is a little apart from the others. That one on his own seems to be talking. At any rate, his lips are moving but there is no one nearby to catch what he is saying. If we draw nearer, we hear what he is saying. *"Father, if it is Your will, remove this cup from Me; nevertheless not My will, but Yours, be done."*[39]

Your will be done. That's really all we can say in our prayers. Your will be done. For we do not truly know what is good for us, and we often ask for what God does not wish us to have. It does not matter how many prayers we say, your will be done is the best prayer we can ever say. For it places us entirely in God's hands, and where else ought we to be but in the hands of God?

A formula for praying

Praying is not easy. We have to be taught how to do it. The experts tell us that we must go somewhere on our own and be quiet. We have to remember God's presence with us and so fill our minds with thoughts of his divine majesty

---

[39] Luke 22:42

before we can begin. Once we have begun, there are certain elements which we should include in all our praying.

We start, as is only right and proper, with looking at God, with feasting our eyes upon the vision of his glorious nature. Then we must go on to include in our praying sorrow for our sinful state, thanksgiving for the many benefits we have received from God, and petitions or supplications as well for others as for ourselves.

We are usually told that we shall the more easily remember those four elements which we should include in all our praying if we think of the word "acts" and fit each element to the letters which make it up. So, "a" stands for our adoration of God, in which all our praying has to be rooted and grounded; "c" stands for contrition, for sorrow for our failing God so often; "t" stands for thanksgiving which we include but rarely; "s" stands for supplication, or petition, both on behalf of others and also on our own behalf.

We neglect such advice on how to say our prayers at our peril. We are seldom wiser than our fathers and so it is best to take notice of the accumulated wisdom of the ages. If, therefore, throughout the centuries, people have found that their praying becomes a poor and feeble thing if it does not include those four traditional elements, then we can be sure that our praying also will become a poor and feeble thing if we neglect but one of them.

On the other hand, however, we must never think that all that is necessary for our praying to become a great and glorious part of our lives is for us always to include such elements. If we listen to them the experts on praying will tell us that praying is more than just a part of our lives. Praying is something that involves the whole of our lives, something that affects and is affected by, the whole of our living. For, however carefully we prepare to pray, however much we bear in mind what each letter of the word "acts" should remind us of – there is no doubt that the best preparation for our praying is the sort of life we have been leading since the last time we prayed. The quality of our living determines the quality of our praying.

Very often we find that our praying is dark and difficult. The reason for that may be the fact that by making it so God is testing us, trying to find out whether we will continue to pray under such a difficulty, and continue for the simple reason that he wishes us to pray. But sometimes, and perhaps more often than we realise, our prayers are dark and difficult because the quality of our personal relationships is poor. How can we expect easy and delightful conversation with God if we are not on easy and delightful terms with the people around us? The people around us are very dear to the heart of God and we cannot, therefore, approach near to the heart of God unless the people around us are dear to our heart also. We cannot get on with God if we are not getting on with the people around us.

Very often, on the other hand, we find that praying is easy and delightful, and we rise from our knees feeling good and holy, thinking to ourselves that we must be on fire with love of God. And perhaps we are, in which case we should say a very big thank you to God for giving us such a treat. But such occasions of feeling good and holy after praying should not lead us to think that the occasions when we do not feel good and holy after praying are occasions when our praying has gone badly. In other words, our feelings are a very poor guide as to the worth and quality of our praying.

We, men and women, are made up in such a way that we are always looking over our shoulder at ourselves and trying to see whether we are succeeding. We naturally, therefore, desire to know if we are making progress with our praying. But the only true test of our praying is to ask ourselves, not what are our feelings when we have finished praying, but to ask ourselves this question, is the quality of our living being improved by our praying? There is no other way of finding out the worth of our praying than by taking a critical look at our daily living.

"I have always said that I cannot admit any other criterion of prayer than its effects. The after effects of good prayer are more definite than the prayer itself: I mean a determination to follow God's will, and to care for nothing else, without any reason to be given for the determination." These are the words of one of the masters in the spiritual life, a former abbot of the Roman Catholic monastery of Downside, Dom John Chapman. Dom John Chapman was surely right; there is no other way of testing the quality of our praying except by seeing whether it improves the quality of our living.

The quality of our living determines the quality of our praying. The quality of our praying determines the quality of our living. Both those statements are equally true and together they prove that praying is, or should be, an integral part of our lives. Too often we make the prayers we say in church or in the privacy of our own room a separate part of our existence; they do not spill over as it were into the rest of our day. When we allow that to happen, we are being unfaithful to the example of our Lord and Master.

Look at Jesus in the garden of Gethsemane. Jesus has gone into the garden with his friends. But he leaves Peter and James and John and goes off on his own to pray. He talks with his Father on such terms of intimacy that he pleads for his Father to change his mind. Jesus would not have been able to do that if his life up to that point had not been in accordance with his Father's will.

When Jesus comes back from praying his first word shows that the rest of his life is to be finished according to his Father's will, as he had just learnt in his praying. Jesus had prayed that if it were possible the cup of suffering which he was to drain to the dregs might pass him by. But when it came to the point, and he realised that it was his Father's will for him drain the cup of suffering dry, he was ready to meet the agent of his death. *"Rise, let us be going. See, My betrayer is at hand."*[40] The whole of Jesus' mortal life had made him worthy of his Father's love; his praying enabled him to end his life as his Father wished.

When you pray, therefore, make sure that since the last time you prayed you have tried to centre your life around God's will for you. Do not hope for any other result from

---

[40] Matthew 26:46

your praying than an improvement in the quality of your living. And may it be your care and chief concern to prepare for the next time you pray by living as well as you possibly can so that the rest of your days maybe in harmony with the divine plan.

Prayer is not easy

"When you pray, go into your room, shut the door, and pray to your Father who is in secret."[41] Three short commands those; and trustworthy guidelines for our prayers. But are they as easy to carry out as they are to read?

Go into a room by yourself. Jesus is telling us to turn away when we pray, turn away from our daily life and towards the Father. But going into a room by ourselves means giving up, for the duration of our praying, our pleasures in life, our interests, our loved ones, our friends – giving all that up to concentrate upon God.

That is the first obstacle in the way of praying. Do we really want to give up so much, even for the short time we usually spend on praying? It seems a heavy price to pay, but if we believe in praying it is a price we shall gladly pay. In order to concentrate on our praying, we have to give up everyone and everything.

Jesus tells us that after we have gone into a room by ourselves, we must then shut the door. A closed door helps keep a room quiet, keeps out the noises made by the rest of the household, helps keep out the din and rattle of the world outside. Jesus warns us to shut the door for fear of distractions, to keep our thoughts from wandering.

There is probably not one of us whose thoughts do not wander when we pray. We settle ourselves to pray, and almost immediately we often start thinking about something else. That great Spanish Saint, Theresa of Avila, suffered from wandering thoughts: she had a vivid phrase for them, she called them "little gnats".

---

[41] Matthew 6:6

It is not surprising that our minds wander when we pray: we are not used to thinking so much about God. The only way to deal with wandering thoughts is to shut the door every time it bursts open. Wandering thoughts are not sin but they become sinful if we allow them to break our concentration upon God.

When we have gone into a room by ourselves and shut the door, Jesus tells us to pray to our Father who is in that secret place. That is not always easy to do. If we could only see our Heavenly Father, we would then find it so much easier to pray; but our Father is in secret, and so often, it seems, in the secret of darkness in which we cannot find him.

Or, as the lady Julian of Norwich said, there was a bitter wind blowing on the day they crucified Christ; and that wind has never stopped blowing in our souls at times, chilling them through and through.

Why do our souls seem to become cold and without feeling when we pray? The "dark night of the soul"[42] is as vivid a phrase as it is true and common. Why is it that when we pray, we often seem to be peering into the darkness in which we cannot see anything, not even the least traces of the divine presence?

Our reaction when praying seems to be going badly tells God, and us, a great deal about how much we want him. Persevering with praying when praying does not seem to be leading anywhere, when it does not make us feel any different, shows how much we are really longing for God and intending to find him. God does not value our praying because it makes us feel good but because it shows that we are in earnest about him.

Go into a room by yourself. Shut your door. Pray to your Father who is there in the secret place. Three short commands, not so easy to carry out as to read but carrying them out will take us a long way on our road back to God.

---

[42] "Dark night of the Soul" is a poem written by the 16th century Spanish mystic and poet St John of the Cross

Prayer without ceasing: a life lived in obedience to God

At a harvest festival the minister was talking to tiny tots about various items of fresh produce on display. He showed them potatoes, brussel sprouts, cabbages, and carrots. He then asked them if they knew one word that would cover all those different items. One little lad was so certain he knew the answer that he shouted out, "Gravy!".

Words *are* slippery things, and it's not always easy to say exactly what they mean. St Paul, for example, advised the Thessalonians to pray without ceasing.[43] It takes some time to work out what he meant. Life today is so hectic and the pressures upon us all so heavy and various that at first Paul's advice seems totally unrealistic. So, it is vitally important to work out what Paul meant by his advice to pray without ceasing.

Behind Paul's advice about prayer are two great truths about God. First, God is Almighty, King of Kings, Lord of Lords, the only Ruler of princes and VIPs, and from his throne he beholds all the dwellers on earth. A German theologian[44] was expressing that truth about God when he described him as the "Holy Other", so utterly different from us his creatures.

Second, God who created the world and everything and everyone in it, he who is Lord of heaven and earth, is yet at the same time very near to each and every one of us. For, in God we live and move and have our being. An early English writer memorably said: "God is our being, and in God we are what we are; not only by cause and being, but also God is in us our cause and our being." Or again, as the lady Julian of Norwich put it: "God is nearer to us than our own soul, for He is the ground in whom our soul standeth."

Obviously, there is a tension between those two great truths about God, a tension vital for our own Christian

---

[43] 1 Thessalonians 5:16

[44] Rudolf Otto 1869-1937

progress. It's the second truth that may help us understand Paul's advice to pray without ceasing. For praying is recognising, acknowledging, God who is always with us and in us. Prayer is stopping for a moment to be conscious of that God in whom we live and move and have our being – rather like drawing deep breaths of the air which always surrounds us and enables us to live. Prayer is the opportunity to realise over and over again, until we no longer have to think consciously about it, for it determines the whole of our approach to life, the grand fact that we already have a relationship with God.

Two practical consequences arise out of our already existing relationship with God. First, prayer requires effort, just as any personal relationship requires effort – it's impossible to get to know anybody in any worthwhile way unless we spend time and effort upon them as well as simply listening to them. On the other hand, prayer does not require entirely or only effort and hard work – part of prayer is just resting in God, as part of any relationship is simply being still and quiet in the company of the other person. "Companionable silence" is a great strengthener with God as in our human relationships.

Part of prayer is therefore allowing ourselves to be carried as it were by God, allowing God to pick us up when we fall. When effort fails and we don't know what to say to him or how to pray at all, and the whole business of prayer seems to be without meaning, as sometimes our earthly relationships seem to be going nowhere, then it means acknowledging that God himself prays for us and in us - as Paul said in another place: "*the Spirit himself intercedes for us, with groanings too deep for words* ".[45]

The second consequence of the right idea about God's nearness to us and in us, is that there has to be a particular time of prayer, specific acts of prayer, occasions when, as in any relationship, we give our whole attention to God, when we concentrate upon him present with us, present in us,

---

[45] Romans 8:26

86

times when we set ourselves consciously to bring our wills, our thinking, more completely into line with his will.

Of course, prayer should not be limited to already organised times of prayer, to the specific acts of prayer that we have already decided upon. For God is still there, with us, in us, guarding and caring for us, even when we do not remember him or are barely conscious of him. One of the best ways to make progress in prayer is to build up the realisation that in God we live and move and have our being, that "Christ in us and we in Christ" is still true even when in our occupations and pre-occupations we seem to have forgotten all about God.

Paul was addressing his advice to pray without ceasing to the ordinary people of Thessalonica city. He had already urged them to work hard at a good honest job of manual labour. Then, without any sense of contradiction on his part, he urged them to pray without ceasing. Clearly, Paul is not referring to various single acts of prayer, different occasions of praying. Rather he is thinking of the whole Christian way of life, of prayer not in terms of words or acts or times but of prayer as a disposition of the will, as an attitude of mind, as a life lived in obedience to God.

To pray without ceasing means, therefore, to live as much as we possibly can in the knowledge and consciousness of God within us as well as God beyond us. In other words, Paul was concerned that we live the whole of our lives in the acknowledged circumstance of a pre-existent relationship between God and ourselves – it is as though he were saying that our various acts of prayer are simply stopping for a moment or two in time to be conscious of that eternal relationship with the God in whom we live and move and have our being.

There is still a problem about that second consequence of the right idea about God, the fact that there have to be particular times of prayer. Just how many such times can we fit into our already busy, chaotic, disorganised days? Perhaps the answer is not to try to fit so many such times into our lives as to use the events of our lives, the things that have happened to us as opportunities for prayer. There are, for example, so many opportunities for Thanksgiving – the dawning of a lovely day, coming up on a wonderful view, an unexpected present, help received, support given – so many thanks possible to God straightaway on the spot as it were for what we receive and enjoy. So many opportunities also for intercession – as awkward customers bump into us at work, in the street, at home: who knows what troubles they have? A quick prayer to God for them may work wonders. Then there are all those on the sick list, the departed, prayers for peace in the world as we read the newspaper or watch the television news. So many opportunities also for contrition or confession or penitence – we are always doing something wrong, always falling short of the target God sets us: an immediate "sorry, God" is the best pick me up.

Pray, therefore, without ceasing – live the whole of your life in the attitude of mind of "Christ in us and we in Christ". Don't bother over much about fitting too many different times of prayer into your busy lives but use as many of the things that happen to you as opportunities for bringing God into the equation as it were. On the other hand, if people can listen to their music as they are walking or jogging, washing up or doing the housework, reading a book or mowing the lawn, or doing anything that doesn't require the whole of their mental activity or attention, then we can't deny that there are indeed many times possible for specific acts of prayer.

"*Pray without ceasing*". Once we have unravelled something of its meaning, the phrase gives us sound advice for our Christian living.

Prayers of supplication

Common Worship is the form of liturgy which is used most often today in Anglican churches. The Book of Common Prayer, compiled by Thomas Cranmer in the sixteenth century and modified in 1662, is the traditional Anglican service book and is still in use today. The Book of

Common Prayer has been, and continues to be, loved for the beauty of its language which is dignified and memorable, but which always speaks to our human condition.

The Book of Common Prayer collects for the day deal with an amazing variety of subject matter. It is remarkable upon how many topics they touch. It is no less remarkable that upon each topic they have something of profound importance to teach us. But before we take a look at one collect in particular, we need to remind ourselves what a collect is. This is because collects appear not only in the Book of Common Prayer and also in Common Worship but also in the liturgies of many other Christian denominations.

A collect is a prayer. Most collects begin with a statement relating to one of God's particular attributes. That statement is then developed into a petition appropriate to the day, linked to the Scripture readings for the day. In addition to their use in public worship, they form a valuable resource for the prayers of the individual Christian.

The Book of Common Prayer collect of the 9th Sunday after Trinity reads as follows:

"Grant to us, Lord, we beseech thee, the spirit to think and do always such things as may be rightful; that we, who cannot do any thing that is good without thee, may by thee be enabled to live according to thy will; through Jesus Christ our Lord. Amen."

This collect gives us the Christian view of life and, within the space of a single sentence, makes three points of great significance about that view. The collect for the 10th Sunday after Trinity tells us something equally important about praying. The collect reads as follows:

"Let thy merciful ears, O Lord, be open to the prayers of thy humble servants; and that they may obtain their petitions make them to ask such things as shall please thee; through Jesus Christ our Lord. Amen."

The collect provides us, among other points, with the answer to a question which is always being asked about praying. It makes no attempt to cover every problem which arises when we pray, but it helps us to settle our mind over one of the problems about praying which is continually being thrust under our noses.

The problem in praying with which we are constantly being faced occurs when we engage in that part of praying which is known as asking or as supplication. It is the problem which is often put to us by sincere and devout Christians. Those sincere and devout Christians have been taught that whatever they ask for in the name of Jesus Christ will be granted to them. And so, confident in what they have been taught, they ask for something in the name of Jesus and are bitterly disappointed when God does not grant that prayer. Their cry goes up, why, oh Lord, why have you not answered my prayer? And after that cry, disappointment sets in, and sometimes they are disillusioned and lose their faith. It is very hard to persuade such people that they have no reason for forsaking their faith.

The reason why such people should not lose their faith when their prayer does not seem to have been granted is the fact that God's ears are always open to our prayers. That is the first important point which the collect for the 10th Sunday after Trinity makes. "Let thy merciful ears, O Lord, be open to the prayers of thy humble servants." We need not bother ourselves over the way in which the collect begins. We can rest assured that God's ears are always open to our prayers. That we ask for his ears to be open is only the common courtesy of not presuming to take for granted something of which we are already certain. God's ears are never closed to our prayers. We begin the collect by asking for them to be open only as a way of engaging his attention.

It should be a great relief to us to know that God is always ready to listen to us. In these days we very often have to deal with large organisations and associations in the management of our lives. The trend in modern business and the global economy, for example, is either for firms to merge and become one enormous company, as when the US food giant Walmart acquired Asda or the bank Santander acquired Abbey National, or for one already large firm to take over several smaller firms and acquire what is almost a monopoly in its part of the business world. But in whatever way businesses become larger, the outsider is often at a loss to know how to approach them. The way in has become immensely complicated for anyone who has not already made contacts on the inside.

The same criticism can also be levelled against the various departments of the government, both local and national. The administration of the country's affairs have to be highly organised, otherwise chaos and confusion would reign supreme. Within the organisation of the administration of the country's affairs there is always the danger that bureaucracy might raise its ugly head. The passion for splitting administration into several departments has to be checked and held back if our citizens are not to spend their lives being passed from pillar to post.

We Christians, on the other hand, should rejoice and be happy because we have a permanent way of easy and open access to the "CEO", so to speak, in our lives. Without help from God our lives quickly fall into pieces and disintegrate. There are, therefore, countless occasions on which we have recourse to God. But whenever we wish to speak with him, we do not have to approach through a host of lesser officials. We can go straight to him and lay our problem directly before him. That is the first important point which the collect for the 10th Sunday after Trinity makes, that God is always accessible to us, that God's ears are always open to our prayers.

But the collect does not only make the point that God's ears are always open to our prayers, it also makes the point that God's predisposition is to grant us what we ask. For God is not only ready to listen to us, he is also eager to give us what we want. If his ears are open to our prayers, his hands are open to shower us with every blessing. As the collect for the 12th Sunday after Trinity puts it, "God is always more ready to hear us than we are to pray to him, and he is wont to give us more than either we desire or deserve." In the words of the collect for the 10th Sunday after Trinity, not only are God's ears never closed to our prayers, but they are also merciful, prejudiced in our favour. We cannot ask him to give us anything that is good without his having already desired to give it to us.

Our Lord once told a story to illustrate God's open handedness. He compared God's open-handedness with a man's open handedness. As our Lord told it, it was an amazing story because while God is always more than ready to satisfy our requests, the man in the story only gave his friend what he wanted because of his audacity in asking what he asked for and at the time when he asked for it. This is the story.[46]

Our Lord said, "*Suppose one of you has a friend who comes to him in the middle of the night and says, My friend, lend me three loaves, for a friend of mine on a journey has turned up at my house, and I have nothing to offer him*"; and he replies from inside, "*Do not bother me. The door is shut for the night; my children and I have gone to bed; I cannot get up and give you what you want*".

Our Lord's comment upon that episode was as follows. "*I tell you that even if he will not provide for him out of friendship, the very shamelessness of the request, in asking for only three loaves to set before a hungry traveller and having woken somebody up in the middle of the night to do so, will make that someone get up and give him all he needs.*" And our Lord went on to point out that what the man did for his unwanted caller for no other reason than that the man had had the audacity to call upon him when he did and upon such an errand, God is always more than ready to do for his friends. And he is prepared to do more besides. For God's bounty does not keep itself within the limits of our request. As our Lord went on to say, earthly fathers, bad as they are, know how to give their children what is good for them. Since that is so, he remarked, how much more will the Heavenly Father give what is good to those who ask him?[47]

---

[46] Luke 11:5-8

[47] Luke 11:13

The third point which the collect for the 10th Sunday after Trinity makes about praying is perhaps the most important one of them all. Many people do not need to be reassured about the first point. They are already convinced, and nothing can shake their belief that they will never be prevented from approaching God. As time goes on, however, doubts begin to creep in about God's willingness to grant our prayers. Time after time our prayers seem to remain unanswered, we say to ourselves that it is no good our being always able to approach God if God never answers our prayers. If God never answers our prayers what point is there in approaching him? The answer to that question is not very easy. I think it is to be found in a story of which I am very fond. I have already told this story, but it is such a good story that it will bear repetition. Here it is.

There was a little girl who very much wanted a doll for Christmas. It was an expensive doll and unfortunately the little girl's parents could not possibly afford to buy it for her. However, the little girl did not know that and, as is the way with little girls, long before Christmas she began to tell God about the doll which she wanted and to ask him to give it to her. Well, Christmas came, and Christmas went but no doll appeared. The little girl's mother was very worried. She did not know how her daughter would take the fact that God did not seem to have answered her prayer. It took the mother some time to pluck up her courage and ask her daughter if she was not terribly disappointed that God had not answered her prayer for a doll. Imagine, therefore, the mother's surprise when her little girl turned to her and said indignantly, "But, Mummy, he did answer my prayer, he said no!".

That is the third point which the collect for the 10th Sunday after Trinity makes. God's ears may never be closed to our prayers. His hands may ever be open to give us what is good for us. But we, for our part, must always have an open mind about our requests for him. In our ignorance we may ask for something which would harm us and would be bad for us if God were to give it to us. And that note of caution, that note of warning about our prayers is continually being sounded in our ears. It is contained, for example, in the prayer which precedes the Grace, in which we ask God to fulfil the desires and petitions of his children, as may be most expedient for them. For we must never assume that God will automatically say yes to every request. In order that we may obtain our petitions, our prayers must contain such requests as shall please him. We should not hold God so cheaply that we make him into a rubber stamp, asking him to grant our requests without thinking about them.

The collect for the 10th Sunday after Trinity is only a short collect but it is full of meaning. It has three important lessons to teach us about that part of our praying which we call supplication or asking. It teaches us, first, that God's ears are always open to our prayers. It teaches us also that God's hands are always open to give us what is good for us. It teaches us, finally, that we, for our part, must always have an open mind about what we are asking for.

The Jesus prayer: no special training needed

A person's name is closely bound up with the person whose name it is. That is why the New Testament uses the name of Jesus to mean Jesus himself. It was in Jesus' name that the disciples performed miracles and exorcisms – they did so, that is, by means of his power. In his name also they baptised – through their actions done in his name Jesus brought people into relationship with himself.

St Paul insists that Jesus' name is absolutely essential for us to be children of God. He tells us that we have to venerate and respect Jesus' name above all other names. St Paul's advice is probably the origin of a delightful custom started in the Middle Ages when medals stamped with the first three letters of Jesus' name were given to the newly baptised.

Since a person's name is an inseparable part of that person, we ought always to use people's names in love, never in anger. To use a person's name lovingly is to acknowledge the worth and dignity of that person, and in so doing we make ourselves better people. When we say a person's name in anger we belittle that person and make ourselves small and mean.

There is a fine old custom of bowing the head every time we say or hear the name of Jesus. That is an outward sign of our respect and love for Jesus. The actual movement of the head is, of course, worthless if we are not living by the inner conviction that Jesus is Lord. Bowing the head in the presence of a temporal sovereign has to be accompanied by inward respect: bowing the head in honour of the King of Kings shows that we believe Jesus is supreme.

The great Orthodox Churches of the East have a wonderful prayer centred on Jesus' name: they call it the "Jesus prayer". No special training or gift is needed before we can use that prayer. Simply settle yourself into a comfortable position. Do not hunch yourself forward but set your shoulders well back so that the air can get into your lungs. Then close your eyes: breathe in slowly several times so as to relax yourself and then begin saying Jesus' name; say it in adoration and love, say his name over and over again, breathing slowly, deeply, and regularly all the time.

The full form of the Jesus prayer is as follows: – "Lord Jesus Christ, Son of God, have mercy on me". We can, of course, shorten that prayer, to "Lord Jesus Christ", even just "Lord Jesus". Countless people down the ages have found the Jesus prayer a wonderful prayer – use it regularly and often, and you will find it a marvellous way of deepening your faith and improving your relationship with Jesus.

"Lord Jesus Christ, Lord Jesus, Lord Jesus". Set aside time for Jesus every day. Repeat his name slowly, again and again and again, in love and adoration; and more and more will you come to love him without whom our lives are poor and mean but with whom and in whom we find fulfilment.

Meditation and contemplation: a way to pray

The other day I was waiting in Market Weighton surgery to see the nurse practitioner. On the wall opposite was a drawing of the new surgery. It is to be called "Market Weighton Health Centre". I began walking to the nurse practitioner's room, and I stirred things up a bit. "You know," I said, "if you're going to call your new place Market Weighton Health Centre, I'm going to rename All Saints' Parish Church, "All Saints' Health Centre". After all, you medical people concern yourself with a particular range of health problems but the Church is concerned with all health issues."

The Church set up hospitals and infirmaries before the State. In doing so the Church has been true to her Lord and Master. Jesus was concerned about our total well-being – he healed the sick in body and mind: and he was just as passionate about we call our spiritual health. After all, he's the Son of the Father who made us, and the Father wants all of us to be sound and well in every way.

Bodily and mental health is important but there are other health concerns to be addressed. When I was a parish priest people came to me to make their confession, that is, to say sorry for what they had done wrong in the presence of one of God's accredited representatives and to hear on his lips the words of Jesus' forgiveness. Nearly all of them, after they had made their confession, were eager for talk, talk about themselves and their relationship with God; and then they went back to the business of their daily lives. From their confession they were getting something they needed very much and that was help with the whole of their lives.

The world of today is very pressurised and increasingly secular. In order to escape the day to day stresses and strains it seems that a growing number of people are becoming interested in creating some space for themselves often by using meditation and contemplation techniques. I am aware of the benefits of meditation and contemplation, and I have met Christians of a variety of denominations who feel the same.

Now putting aside time for meditation and contemplation is sometimes referred to as "me time". Now, "me time" sounds selfish but people who refer to meditation and contemplation in this way are not being selfish. These people are usually all busy people – in their families, at work, and in what little leisure time they have: they know something is missing from their lives. These people are those who are eager for the practical sessions on meditation and contemplation. These practical sessions show them how to become still and quiet. In fact, I am often told that in those sessions they feel that their batteries are being recharged and their energy levels are topped up. As a Christian priest I would like to take those practical meditation and contemplation sessions further and use the techniques of becoming still and quiet as a way of focusing upon God. I'm grateful to a member of a recent congregation who gave me the other day an excellent slogan for the Christian practice of meditation: switch off from the world, switch on to God.

There is a story about two brothers. The brothers were always in trouble, at home, at school, and with the police. One Sunday, in sheer desperation, their parents took them to church. Of course, they sat at the back of the church. The vicar went into the pulpit. Now he was a dramatic type of person. He began by whispering: "We've lost God". He said that several times, each time more loudly. Finally, he roared out, "We've lost God", and thumped the pulpit. Silence followed, and in that silence one brother turned to the other and said, "They've lost God: let's get out of here before they pin it on us."

God is largely lost today, and it's mainly because the Church today does not do very much teaching about meditation and contemplation. Instead, diocesan and other advisors urge us to go on courses, attend discussion or buzz groups, even go away for bonding weekends. I even heard fellow clergy say that there's not much time for meditation and contemplation: there are so many practical issues to deal with!

But remember what the Psalmist said, "*Be still and know that I am God*".[48] And it was, of course, the invaluable practice of a young man, utterly and absolutely devoted to his Heavenly Father, to build into his daily life regular and

---

[48] Psalm 46:10

habitual periods of time when he was alone and still and focused upon God: without those times that young man would never have been able to go to his death on the cross.

Meditation or contemplation has been described as not asking God for things but simply looking at God and letting God look at us. That form of prayer is not an optional extra in the Christian life: it is a vital necessity. It is tremendously important for our total well-being, bodily as well as otherwise – witness the references we can find to the fact that meditation helps bring down our blood pressure. "*Be still and know that I am God*" and take Jesus' regular practice of time spent alone with God, focusing entirely upon God alone as a model and pattern in our own lives.

The Bible

We are, firstly, the people of a man – Christians, Christ's people. But we are also the people of the book, biblical people, the people of the Bible. For without the Bible there can be no Christianity. Take the Bible away, destroy every copy of it, erase its memory from our minds so that it will be as if it had never existed – and the Church will not exist much longer. By the Church I do not mean ecclesiastical buildings but the Christian community – we could not remain devoted to Christ, have the right ideas about him, if we did not have the Bible to refer to.

It is perhaps difficult for us to imagine ourselves scriptureless, to picture what life would be like without the Bible. Holy Scripture is so woven into the fabric of our religious life that we hardly notice its presence. We are scarcely aware, for example, how much the Bible and phrases from it underpin the service of Holy Communion, not to mention the services of Morning and Evening Prayer, both services which ought to perhaps to be as much part of our daily lives as our individual prayer.

We are so familiar, then, with the Bible that we are barely aware of it any longer. Let us take a fresh look at it, therefore, and remind ourselves what an extraordinary book it is.

The first surprise about the Bible is that its second part is so full of quotations from the first part. The New Testament is full of phrases from the Old Testament. Time after time in the New Testament we read, for example, the phrase, "this took place that the Scriptures might be fulfilled". We call those references "proof texts", quotations from the Old Testament put into the New Testament to show that God had Christianity in mind long before Christ appeared on earth.

In one way, of course, it is no surprise that the early Church in Jerusalem, living as it did in the heart of Judaism, in the centre of Old Testament belief, refers to the Old Testament so often. It was an excellent strategy on the part of the Christians in Jerusalem to point out that what had taken place in the life and death and resurrection of Jesus had all been hinted at, foreshadowed in the Old Testament.

On the other hand, it was not long before the Christian message moved out of Jerusalem, into the wider, non-Jewish, Gentile world, a world which knew little of the Old Testament, a world in which the Old Testament played no part. And yet, in that wider world the early Christians made no move to get rid of those many Old Testament references, they had no desire to expunge the Old Testament from the pages of the New Testament. It seems that the Old Testament quotations in the New Testament were so moving in themselves – as we are moved by quotations from poetry – that they impressed themselves upon the minds of the Gentiles as being especially significant, particularly worthwhile. In other words, the Jews had said something in matters religious which no other people in the world had said. The Scriptures spoke to men and women with authority, almost as Shakespeare, for example, does to people of little faith or no belief today – and that authority, the Gentile Christians realised, was not human, not rational only: it was inspired. These are Holy Scriptures, worthy therefore of our utmost attention, demanding constant and diligent study.

We have to grasp one more important point about the New Testament writings. Most of them are occasional pieces of writing. The books of the New Testament are not systematic treaties about God in Jesus – they were each written at a particular time and for a particular purpose. Take St Paul's letters: St Paul wrote each letter to a particular group of people, in a particular place, with a particular purpose in mind – for example to Christians in Corinth, in Rome, in Thessalonica saying something different to each group. On the other hand, there is no doubt but that the recipients of those letters passed them on for other people to read, and rightly so because the letters make points important to all of us.

There is a further point about the New Testament writings. We approach them the wrong way round. We tend to read the Gospels first and then the letters, as if the letters are a commentary on the Gospels, and simply draw out the meaning of the Gospels. As a matter of fact, the letters came first in time and the Gospels later. The Gospels are, in fact, supplementary to the letters, and we ought to read the letters first to see their implications for us of our religion in the world, then read the Gospels to "back up" what the letters say.

It is also interesting to note that it was almost as an afterthought that the New Testament writings were added to the Holy Scriptures of the Jews to form what we now call the Bible. St Luke was one of the latest New Testament writers; and perhaps he had some idea that he was writing Holy Scripture. St Paul and St Mark, however, do not seem to have had any such idea. And, their writings were not the only books put out for Christians to read in the early days of the Church – there were very many more. An excellent test sorted out those books that now go to make up the Bible, the test of repetition. By the end of the second century A.D. the different Churches were reading, independently of one another, more or less the same books – some books had stood the test of time, others had not: the same sort of process is going on today with hymns. Many are written, few will last.

The Book of Common Prayer collect for the 2nd Sunday in Advent[49] tells us that we have to hear, read, mark, learn, and inwardly digest the Scriptures. *Hearing* the Scriptures is no problem, if we come to church. Not only do we have extracts from the Bible read aloud – Old Testament reading, Epistle, Gospel - but the whole service is a pattern or mosaic of words and phrases from the Bible.

Reading the Bible is no problem either. Copies of the Bible are cheap enough in paperback and in digital form, and these days we may take our pick of which version we prefer.

Marking the Bible is easy – all we need is a pencil or pen (or electronic equivalent), in order to underline or write in the margin. After all, better a Bible well-thumbed and written in than a Bible well-bound and never used.

We are also to *learn* the Scriptures. The old-fashioned habit of learning by heart, committing to memory, is still enormously valuable. Such learning gives us a rich store of information and thoughts to draw on, at any time, when we do not have a copy of the Bible to hand, in the garden, on a walk, in the bath, in the kitchen. If we have already learnt them, it is also easier to digest the Scriptures, easier, that is, to keep turning them over in our mind, to ponder them, to get as much out of them as we possibly can. The true Christian, the growing Christian, is the person whose knowledge of the Bible is always increasing.

These days, of course, there is a problem in reading the Bible, a problem that earlier times don't seem to have been aware of. The problem of how much of the Bible is true, how much of it we can accept. After all, so the argument goes, the New Testament writers thought very differently from the way we do today; they had very different backgrounds and that affected their picture of Jesus, what they believed about

---

[49] Blessed Lord, who hast caused all Holy Scriptures to be written for our learning. Grant that we may in such wise hear them, read, mark, learn, and inwardly digest them, that by patience and comfort of thy holy word, we may embrace and ever hold fast the blessed hope of everlasting life, which thou hast given us in our Saviour Jesus Christ. Amen.

him. We, with our different ways of looking at things, cannot always go along therefore with what the New Testament writers said; and some biblical scholars seem to leave us with very little in the Bible to accept as important and true for all time about Jesus.

But biblical studies seem to reflect what goes on in literary studies in general. First of all, there was the text, what the author wrote, and the task was to understand the text, to find out what the author intended. Then people began to say that it was not the text itself, produced at some time in the past, whenever that time was, that was important but how the reader responds to the text in his or her own time. After all, the argument ran, we all come to a text or book with our own stores of experience and knowledge and our own ways of looking at things. No one, therefore, can be expected to read a book in exactly the same way as anyone else. Thus, the reader's response to the text became all important and not the text itself.

It was not long, however, before scholars and literary critics – some of them, at any rate – began to see where that would lead, to rampant individualism, to the exaltation of the reader's response over anything the author intended or wrote, to there being as many texts, as it were, as there are people studying them. Therefore, the scholars hit upon the idea of "the competent reader", and making such a reader's response the normal response, what we all ought to find in the text.

Here life becomes difficult – no one seems able to agree about what makes a competent reader. It is not surprising therefore, that there is in both biblical and literary studies a return to the text itself, an attempt to find out what the text means. In fact, if we do not do that in biblical studies, we may be guilty of more than rampant individualism – we may be guilty of idolatry, each one of us making each our own God in our own image, if we simply interpret the Bible according to our very own whims and fancies.

I remember what a friend of mine once said. George Thompson was the vice principal of my theological college in Salisbury. He also produced a commentary on Luke's Gospel in the Oxford Clarendon Series as well as a commentary on the pastoral letters for the Cambridge University Press, plus numerous articles in various learned journals. George Thompson was once a pupil of perhaps the earliest of the radical theologians, Dennis Mincham. George Thompson once said to me of Dennis Mincham: "I do wish that Dennis would not be so negative about the Bible, content to point out how much of it, with his 20th century ways of thinking, he cannot swallow. I wish he would ask instead a far more important question, why, with their different ways of thinking, the New Testament writers thought it important to write what they did about Jesus. That way," George Thompson said, "we shall be able to get more out of the Bible."

Fashions change in everything. We call ourselves Christians, Christ's people; and we are also the people of the book. If we cannot find any permanent truth in the Bible there will be no one Jesus to hold his people together. We shall be making, each one in our own time, our own Jesus, and the Bible will become useless as a book of universal Christian reference. Yet we believe that it was to free us from our selfish and self-centred individualism that Jesus came to save us. He can still do that if, in the community of the Church, under the guidance of the Holy Spirit, we set ourselves to read, mark, learn, and inwardly digest those same Holy Scriptures, to his glory and for our salvation.

Questions for discussion or reflection

- *How often do you pray?*
- *What are your prayer techniques?*
- *Do you ever find it difficult to pray? Why is this?*
- *Did any of the suggested prayer techniques in this chapter resonate with you and if so, why?*
- *How good is your knowledge of the Bible? What can you do to improve or increase your knowledge?*

Lord's Prayer

The Lord's Prayer is the prayer for which most people, whether or not they identify as Christians, know the words. In fact, many of us probably do not actually remember learning the words to the Lord's Prayer. The words are something which we always seem to have been able to recite. This prayer, the Lord's Prayer, is the one our Lord taught us. However, how many of us have actually stopped to consider what each petition in the prayer means? This chapter does just that.

The two versions of the Lord's Prayer

There are two versions of the Lord's Prayer in the New Testament: Matthew's is one,[50] Luke's the other[51]. Matthew's version is longer than Luke's – Luke begins simply with "Father", not "our Father", and he leaves out "who art in heaven", "thy will be done, on earth as in heaven", and "but deliver us from evil".

Matthew and Luke also introduce the Lord's Prayer differently. Matthew talks about almsgiving, prayer, and fasting, and then gives his version of the Lord's Prayer. Luke tells us that Jesus was praying and when he'd finished one of the disciples said to him, "Lord, teach us how to pray."

Luke's version of Lord's Prayer maybe nearer to what Jesus originally taught. That does not mean we have to ignore Matthew's version. Both versions come from what Jesus said about how to pray, and both were used from the very earliest days of the Church. The versions were used in two different places – Christians in Galilee used Matthew's version, Christians in Jerusalem used Luke's. However, both versions show how important Jesus' teaching on prayer was, and the differences do not really matter that much.

---

[50] Matthew 6:5-15

[51] Luke 11:1-13

The Lord's Prayer does not always end in the same way. We sometimes add, "for thine is the kingdom, the power and the glory". Neither Matthew nor Luke have those words. What happened was this. Early Christians, using the prayer the Lord had taught, felt compelled to break out into his praise. They were so grateful for the Lord's Prayer, and for the Lord's goodness, that they could not but add such heartfelt words about the nature of God.

A last word. Just before he introduces the Lord's Prayer Matthew issues a warning about prayer in general. The Authorised Version translates this as warning against "vain repetitions". The Revised Standard Version is slightly better with its warning against "empty words". The Greek word Matthew actually uses is vivid and graphic. It referred originally to stammering or stuttering – "g g g g g good m m m m morning". The repeated g and m don't mean anything until we know the meaning of the whole word.

Matthew is warning against us gabbling our prayers, or saying prayers without meaning them, or of uttering words whilst our minds are elsewhere. When we pray with sincerity and meaning then the more often we say a prayer the better, especially when that prayer is the Lord's Prayer, the prayer our dear Lord himself gave us.

The structure of the Lord's Prayer

Trouble began early in the infant Church. People believed that Christ would return in a short time and God's everlasting kingdom would then begin. But some Christians didn't see the point of doing any work, therefore, in that short interim period. St Paul had harsh words[52] for them – if you don't work, you don't eat. Paul had no time for spongers.

We do not have any sense of urgency about Christ's coming again today. We pay lip service to the belief but it is gone to the back of our minds, and we don't behave as though Christ will return any time soon. That's why we do not say the Lord's Prayer as the early Christians said it, not

---

[52] 2 Thessalonians 3:10

only as a daily prayer but as a prayer for a sure to come future.

For the early Christian was keenly aware that Christ would come again. Hallowed be your name. Your kingdom come. Your will be done. Asking God to usher in his everlasting rule. The request for bread is also a request for the bread of life or heavenly manna of the last days. "Forgive us our trespasses" will of course refer to the final judgement at the end of all time, not just a decision on a day's events. "Lead us not into temptation" is also a plea that we may escape the trouble that Luke tells us will come just before God's kingdom arrives.

The Lord's Prayer works superbly in two ways, therefore, as a prayer for the future as well as a prayer for today. Christ may not yet have come for the second time, but we simply do not know how long present time will last. We have to get ready for the end of time – and the Lord's Prayer is a very necessary help and reminder.

The structure of the Lord's Prayer has much to teach us. It is a two-part structure. The first part has to do with God; the second part with us. That two-part structure sets the pattern for all our praying. Praying is when we turn our minds to God. That is our first duty when we pray, to fix our attention upon God first of all; and the pattern of the Lord's Prayer shows that we should spend nearly half of our prayer time on God. Most of us, of course, spend very little time on God before we start bombarding him with our demands and requests.

Another point. All of the pronouns in the second half of the prayer are plural. "Our, us, we". We cannot pray the Lord's Prayer without thinking of other people. A selfish or solitary Christian is a contradiction in terms. Christians can neither go it alone nor do without other people.

Finally, both Matthew and Luke, after giving us the Lord's Prayer, say something about forgiveness. Prayer and forgiveness have always been connected. Christian prayer cannot possibly be effective or be any good if Christians are not at peace with one another. Perhaps that is why the

Church of today can seem to be so weak and prayer seems often ineffective – Christians are at one another's throats as it were: or, if that language sounds exaggerated, a recent writer put it like this, "holy people engaged on holy tasks can be unholily quarrelsome". Christians at peace with one another and working hard in the Lord's service are a mighty power for good in the world.

Our Father which art in heaven: God the Father

We can learn a lot in the most unlikely ways. For five years I was a part-time chaplain at a school for young offenders.[53] I didn't Bible-bash or preach at the boys. My Rector had told me I wouldn't be of any use in the school until I was accepted as part of the furnishings as it were. I therefore played a lot of badminton with the boys.

After one particularly good and hard-fought game of doubles the four of us were chatting together when one of the boys suddenly burst out with, "You know, I can't go along with what you say about God as Father. If God is anything like my father, then he's no bloody good – my father is nearly always drunk and likes nothing better than beating my mother and me up."

Jesus didn't invent the idea of God as Father. The idea is perhaps as old as religion itself. Samarian prayers, for example, 3000 years before Christ came, address God as father. But for Jesus, for the very first time in history, the idea of God as Father was all important. That's why Paul begins more than one of his letters by referring to the grace and peace that comes from God the Father. Paul even says that when we cry, "Abba, Father", that's the voice of God speaking in us. St John, in his gospel is always going on about "the children of God".

Jesus obviously knew many good fathers. Jaerius, whose only daughter was at death's door, begged Jesus to save her. Then there was the father with a lunatic boy, also the father

---

[53] Dad was the part-time chaplain at East Moor Approved School, Adel, Leeds during his curacy.

of the prodigal son. All those men had great love and concern for their children. Not surprisingly, therefore, Jesus tells us that God the Father feeds the birds and cares for fallen sparrows, that it is God the Father's will that no one goes astray, that God the Father gives to those who seek and opens the door to those who knock.

Jesus pushes the idea of God as Father even further. He says that God demands as well as gives. If we are to go to heaven we must do the will of the Father in heaven, we are to become perfect even as the Father in heaven is perfect, we must forgive as the Father forgives. One of the first words a young child learnt at home in Jesus' day was, "Abba" meaning dad or daddy. That's the word Jesus wants us to use when we speak with God – "Abba" because God loves and cares for us, and in his concern for us wants us to behave properly.

Finally, Jesus himself is the living demonstration of what God is like as father. We know this because Jesus draws the closest possible connection between himself and the Kingdom of God. He speaks of the Kingdom of God as the Kingdom of my Father – it is the Father in heaven who has given to Jesus the Kingdom Jesus gives to us. Jesus thanks the Father for what he has shown to the "babes" – and the "babes" include the poor in spirit to whom the Kingdom is promised. On one occasion Jesus told Peter that he was the Messiah, the Son of the living God. Jesus told Peter that flesh and blood have not revealed that to him but "*my Father in heaven*".[54] In other words, Jesus is the living proof of what God is like as Father, and the best demonstration of what the Kingdom of God is like.

Our Father in heaven

We call God the Father, our Father, and we say that he is in heaven. But the first question is – can everyone call God, Father? Some people say that they can. God certainly wishes everyone well, sinners included, that's the opinion of the

---

[54] Matthew 16:17

Gospel writers: but that's very different from everybody in the world being regarded as a child of God.

St Paul says that we are children of God by adoption:[55] we are not God's children by right. Paul is saying that we may become God's children because of God's initiative – God takes the first step towards us.

What Paul says is a bit misleading. We are usually adopted when very young, and we have no say in the matter. But in order to become God's children and call him Father, we have to respond to God's initiative in approaching us which he did in Jesus of Nazareth.

Jesus is God's offer to us to become his children, and we cannot become God's children unless we respond to Jesus. When we do respond to Jesus then we truly become children of God and we can sincerely call God our Father. If we do not call Jesus, Lord, we can't call God our Father.

The second point to note is that God is "our" Father, not "my" Father. Respond to the offer that God makes to us in Jesus and we become members of the community, members of the Church. Christians cannot go it alone: there can be no such person as a Christian on his or her own.

A third point is this: we say that God our Father is in "heaven". We have already learnt to call God, "Abba"; that lovely Aramaic word which means dad or daddy, and our relationship with God is one of the closest intimacy. The word "heaven" reminds us that God is also "the Almighty Other", the "Transcendent One", beyond and above us all.

The word "heaven" finds those two aspects of God together. God, the Almighty Other, God, the Transcendent One, is also lovingly interested in all the details of our daily living – and heaven is no longer far away from us: for Jesus came as the Son of God, bringing heaven within our reach. In Jesus the Kingdom of Heaven is upon us, is at hand, is close by.

"Our Father which art in heaven" – these words are the keynote for the whole prayer. Everything on earth has to be

---

[55] Ephesians 1:5

110

related to, brought in subjection to, referred to, the name, the will of our Father in heaven. Heaven and earth are now brought close together because of Jesus – the Heavenly One is also our Father: the Almighty One is intimate and close – that is what our Blessed Lord and Saviour, Jesus Christ, came into the world to demonstrate.

Hallowed be thy name

"Hallowed be thy name." "Hallowed" means to consecrate or make holy, and the name is God himself. But God is holy. It's difficult for us to see, therefore, how we can pray for God's name to be made holy – what sense can be made of the phrase? The difficulty has been felt for a long time. About 1600 years ago St John Chrysostom made the following suggestion, that "hallowed be thy name" is not a petition or request at all but rather an introductory act of praise. People who have agreed with Chrysostom have quoted, in support of his theory, the well-known Jewish phrase, "the holy one, blessed is he."

But let us consider what the words "hallow" and "name" mean. About the holiness of God there are two points to be made. There is, to begin with, the idea of righteousness, or moral purity, an idea which, even if it was not there at first, is certainly found from the prophets onwards. For example, Isaiah says, *"God who is Holy is sanctified in righteousness."*[56] Leviticus,[57] in the holiness code, says that *"ye shall be holy to Me, for I the Lord am holy"*. It is true that some people think of holiness in external terms only. But increasingly the trend is to think of things, places, practices as holy because they are connected with the worship of the holy God, and God's holiness includes righteousness.

The second point to be made about holiness is that it includes the idea of awefulness, awesomeness, the idea of the numinous, of something, someone, wholly other than us.

---

[56] Isaiah 5:16

[57] Leviticus 19:2

Thus God is holy as a king, of tremendous majesty, as surrounded by a light so blinding that no human can draw near. Holiness is, as it were, God's hidden being: when manifested, it becomes his shining glory. In Isaiah, *"holy, holy, holy is the Lord of hosts: the whole earth is full of his glory."*[58] And we are told that the last of God's works is that *"the Earth shall be filled with the knowledge of the glory of the Lord as the waters cover the sea."*[59]

So much for hallowed. Now, the name. The name is not a label as most names are. The name is God himself. The word "name" was often used to avoid pronouncing the sacred Tetragrammaton, the Hebrew word for God which was written in four letters. Thus, for example, Isaiah says, *"behold, the name of the Lord cometh from afar, burning with his anger"*[60] – when he really means God himself. Similarly, later in Isaiah, *"so shall they fear the name of the Lord from the west, and his glory from the rising of the sun."*[61] Again, Isaiah means God himself. In the New Testament, in Hebrews, *"God is not unrighteous to forget your work... and the love which ye showed towards his name"*[62] – the name is God himself, his totality, his uniqueness, his existence before even the world began and after its completion.

The phrase "hallowed be thy name" puts together the two ideas of holiness and awesomeness. The combination had been common in the Jewish liturgy. Benedictions made up largely of Old Testament phrases, are recited on weekdays at the services in the Jewish synagogue, some of them also on the Sabbath and festivals. They include the phrase, "holy art thou, and dreadful is thy name". Experts on Judaism say that the sanctification of God's name is the most characteristic principle and motive of the Jewish code of

---

[58] Isaiah 6:3

[59] Habakkuk 2:14

[60] Isaiah 30:27

[61] Isaiah 59:19

[62] Hebrews 6:10

behaviour – "God hallows his own name by demonstrating his supreme Godhead and compelling the nations to acknowledge it." The following from Ezekiel[63] is a superb illustration of that: "*thus saith the Lord God: I do this not for your sakes, O house of Israel, but for mine holy name's sake, which ye have profaned among the nations, whither ye want. And I will sanctify my great name... And the heathen shall know that I am the Lord, saith the Lord God when I shall be sanctified in you before their eyes.*"

God hallows his name, therefore, by doing things that lead or constrain us to acknowledge him as God. And as it is God's supreme wish that all mankind shall ultimately own and serve him as the true God, so it is the chief end of Israel to hallow his name by living in such a way that everyone shall see and say that the God of Israel is the true God. The New Testament equivalent of that is the phrase, "*let your light so shine before men, that they may glorify your Father which is in heaven.*"[64]

"Hallowed be thy name". How much is the hallowing of God's name God's business and how much is it ours? Perhaps, at this early point in the Lord's Prayer we are meant to think primarily or chiefly of God, of the time when his name will be universally respected, of the time when God's rule is established over all the world, of the time when everyone acknowledges his holiness. That time is, of course, the future; and the fact is it can only be God's work – we cannot do it. But in the meantime, it is true to say that God is working through us, and the hallowing of God's name lays a tremendous responsibility upon us. We cannot seriously pray "hallowed be thy name" without remembering that God has, as it were, put his good name at risk by putting it into our hands, to hallow or to profane it – if we in the Church do not take God and his name seriously, we cannot expect the rest of the world to do so.

---

[63] Ezekiel 36:22

[64] Matthew 5:16

Thy kingdom come

The Old Testament doesn't have much to say about God's kingdom. But it does emphasise and stress that the Lord is King. Unfortunately, however, not everybody acknowledges that the Lord is King; and so the Jews began to look forward to a time in the future when everyone would acknowledge and honour the Lord as King.

In Jesus' teaching, the Kingdom of God is vitally important: it is absolutely central in everything he had to say about God. Nor does Jesus think of God's Kingdom in any narrow or nationalistic way. Even before Jesus began his ministry, John Baptist had insisted that the Jews, the children of Abraham, would have no preferential position in God's kingdom.

Jesus is even more emphatic on that point. Luke says, people will "*come from East and West, from North and South, and will sit down in the Kingdom of God*".[65] In Matthew, "*the Kingdom of God will be taken away from you [the Jews] and given to a nation bearing the fruits of it*".[66]

Jesus also tells us that the coming Kingdom is God's gift to us. In Luke he is emphatic that "*it is your Father's good pleasure to give you the Kingdom*".[67] In Matthew[68] he goes even further and says that the rewards of the Kingdom do not come in proportion to any work we have done. The stark truth is that we cannot build the Kingdom, nor can we bring the Kingdom about, nor can we calculate the time of its coming. All we can do is to repeat, to watch, and to pray, and hope that we qualify for admission when the Kingdom comes – hope, that is, that we have faith enough and are sorry enough and are willing to receive God's gifts.

There is another new and startling point in Jesus' teaching about the Kingdom. Time and time again Jesus says that the Kingdom is "at hand", "has arrived", "has come upon us".

---

[65] Luke 13:29

[66] Matthew 21:49

[67] Luke 12:32

[68] Matthew 20:1-15

It's equally obvious, however, that the Kingdom is not yet fully here. That's why we have a great paradox in Christianity: we believe that the Kingdom has come: we believe also that it is yet to come.

On the one hand, we speak of the day of the Lord, the victory over evil, the making of all things new. Jesus has made us kings, and already we eat and drink at his table. We inhabit the world of faith and the sacraments. The powers of the new age are already at work. Hence that confidence. On the other hand, the Kingdom has only begun, it is not yet fully here, not completely realised yet. The evil one and wickedness still partly hold the world in thrall and subjugation – Jesus himself warns us of that. We must still wait and pray, both confident and trembling at the same time – for, of course, the Kingdom of God will never fully come if we do not make the Lord king of our lives now.

Thy will be done on earth as it is in heaven

The phrase, "thy will be done on earth as it is in heaven", seems to be repeating the previous phrase, "thy kingdom come". That may be the reason why Luke did not include it in his version of the prayer. Matthew includes it but the question then arises as to why Matthew included it. Matthew's is, of course, the most Jewish of the four gospels, but "thy will be done" is not at all a common phrase in the Jewish liturgy. Perhaps Matthew remembered Jesus' prayer in the garden of Gethsemane when he spoke not of his will being done but the Father's. However, if "thy will be done" is a repetition of "thy kingdom come" it is a repetition with a difference, and that difference is a good reason for taking the phrase as an original part of the prayer.

There is no difficulty about the language of the phrase. It doesn't contain any technical terms like "name" or "kingdom". "Will" means just what it says. The word does not occur often in the Old Testament and when it does it's fairly late on. But the Rabbis often speak of doing the will of the Father in heaven. By the way, "heaven and earth" simply means the whole universe. The Lord's Prayer speaks of "heaven" and not "heavens" because of the Greek background. In Greek, whether the Greek of the Old Testament or the Greek of the New Testament, it makes no difference. In Greek the practice seems to be that when heaven is associated with earth as part of the whole creation then the singular "heaven" is used; the plural form "heavens" refers to the dwelling place of God.

"Thy will be done". We have to be careful how we interpret the phrase. It's easy to point to what seems to be parallel passages in non-Christian writings about accepting the will of God. Ancient philosophers such as Epictetus and Seneca counselled accepting God's will. On closer examination, however, what those writers were advising was something very different from our phrase. Those writers belong to the Platonic stoic tradition and what they were after was fatalistic resignation to whatever happens, a patient acquiescence in what actually takes place.

We belong to the Jewish Christian tradition and that says something very different. We are not so much to will what God wills as to do what God wills; and God reveals or shows his will to us not so much in the happenings and events of human life as in his commandments. The Psalmist may say, *"whatsoever the Lord pleased, that did he in heaven and earth"*.[69] But nowhere does he say that the Lord is pleased with all that happens in heaven and earth – far from it: the Lord is not pleased with all that happens in heaven and earth. What is important for us is not that we should will what happens but that we should do what we ought to. That teaching is common to both the Jewish and the Christian traditions. The Rabbi said, "Lord of the world, we have done what you have appointed for it; do for us what you have promised". The New Testament says, *"not everyone that saith Lord, Lord shall enter the kingdom of heaven but he that doeth the will of my Father in heaven"*.[70] Then again, the true family of Jesus is said to consist of those who do the

---

[69] Psalm 135:6

[70] Matthew 7:21

Father's will.[71] And when we look for the Father's will for us we find it in the Sermon on the Mount[72] and the two great commandments, to love God and to love our neighbours as ourselves.

John's gospel and the New Testament letters often use the phrase "the will of God" to sum up the work of salvation. John has Jesus saying, "*my meat is to do the will of him that sent me and to finish his work*".[73] The writer of the letter to the Hebrews has him saying, "*Lo, I come to do thy will*".[74] St Paul describes his apostolic ministry of bringing people back to God as being carried out "*through the will of God*".[75]

That New Testament use of the phrase "the will of God" brings us up against the same paradox or apparent contradiction that we found in the first two petitions of the Lord's Prayer. The work of salvation has been brought about by what Jesus did – in that sense, God's will has been done: yet we still pray, "thy will be done". We are praying that what is hidden, that what is now known only to faith, may be seen and made clear. When we pray for God's will to be done in heaven as in earth, we are praying for God's will to be done unreservedly, by everyone, everywhere.

An interesting question arises here. Are we to understand that in heaven God's will is already perfectly done but obviously not so done here on earth? That seems to be what the usual translation means – we need only to pray for God's will to be perfectly done on earth. The Jews, however, thought of heaven as created and passing away, rather like earth. And Paul in his letter to the Colossians said that things in heaven need to be reconciled as well as things on earth.[76] He stressed the same point when he wrote to the Philippians that "*in the name of Jesus every knee shall bow, of things in*

---

[71] Matthew 12:50

[72] Matthew 5-7

[73] John 4:34

[74] Hebrews 10:9

[75] 1 Corinthians 1:1

[76] Colossians 1:20

117

heaven and things in earth and things under the earth. "[77] Matthew[78] and the writer of the book of Revelation[79] are quite clear and emphatic that to the risen Christ is given all power in heaven and on earth.

"As in heaven, so on earth". The Bible tells us that heaven and earth are where God carried out his will in creation. It is only right, therefore, that we pray for the final completion of God's will to be carried out in both heaven and earth. Note that the first three petitions of the Lord's prayer deal, first of all, with God's very nature – his holiness and his name – then with his action in his Kingdom – the doing or carrying out of his will – finally with the totality of the sphere in which God's will is to be done.

"Hallowed be thy name", "thy kingdom come", and now "thy will be done, as in heaven so on earth". The third petition gathers the first two petitions together as it were, and extends their range, so to speak, to the utmost conceivable limit. There is to be no place, nowhere, where God's will is not to be done. But, of course, there is no real hope of God's will being done here on earth if we Christians aren't trying to do his will here and now.

Give us today our daily bread

Different things mean different things to different people. Take computers and sex, for example. Women, it is said, tend to look upon computers as masculine for the following reasons:

Firstly, in order to get their attention you have to turn them on. Secondly, they have a lot of data but they are usually clueless. Thirdly, most of the time they are a problem. Fourthly, as soon as you commit yourself to one you realise you could have had a better model if only you'd waited a little longer.

---

[77] Philippians 2:10

[78] Matthew 28:18

[79] Revelation 5:13

Men, on the other hand, it is said, tend to look upon computers as feminine for these four reasons:

Firstly, no one but their creator understands their internal logic. Secondly, the secret language they use to communicate with other computers is incomprehensible to everyone else. Thirdly, even your small mistakes are stored in the memory for later retrieval. Fourthly as soon as you commit yourself to one you find yourself spending half your paycheque on accessories.

That different things mean different things to different people is a fact of life we can usually live with without it causing too much of a problem. Sometimes, however, we just don't know the meaning of something which applies to the phrase in the Lord's Prayer, "give us this day our daily bread". Specifically, we don't know what the original Greek word used to describe the bread actually means. The original Greek word for "daily".

But first, a general remark before we get on to that particular difficulty. Until the petition "give us this day our daily bread", the Lord's Prayer has concentrated on God, on his being, his glory, his action. From now on the Lord's Prayer mentions the needs of mankind. That's perhaps why its format changes – we do not have any more verbs in the passive form: they have the active form: – no longer "hallowed be thy name", "thy will be done" (passive) but "forgive us", "give us this day" (active). The pronouns also change – no longer "thy" ("thy kingdom, thy will"): instead we talk of "us" and "our".

The particular difficulty in the petition "give us this day our daily bread" lies in the meaning of the original Greek word usually translated as "daily". The plain truth of the matter is that nobody is sure what that original Greek word means. It occurs only in New Testament versions of the Lord's Prayer, in patriotic passages which obviously derive from the Lord's Prayer, and perhaps, but only perhaps, in a papyrus document belonging to the second century A.D., found in Upper Egypt, and since then lost so that nobody can now check it. There is also the further difficulty that part of the word was missing in that papyrus: and if scholars completed it correctly, then it may, but only may, be equivalent to a Latin word in a list detailing items of expenditure which was found inscribed on a wall in the buried Roman town of Pompeii, the Latin word *diaria* which means "daily ration".

What an international chase to track down the meaning of the original Greek translated as meaning "daily" in the Lord's Prayer. From Palestine, home of the Lord's Prayer, to Egypt, to southern Italy. And the chase may have been no more than a wild goose chase. But even if we could be certain about the text and meaning of the papyrus that would still not prove that that is what the word meant in first century Palestine.

Origen was a very good Greek scholar, and he emphatically says that he had never come across the word either in learned or in popular speech. Nor do we get much help from other people who lived nearer the spoken Greek of that time than we do. In the eastern part of the Church, the oldest Syriac versions have a word which in Syriac means "continual". The revised version of the Syriac has a word meaning "of our necessity". Of the Egyptian versions the Sahidii version has "coming"; the Memphitic has "of the morrow".

In the Western Church the greatest scholar after Origen was St Jerome who lived between A.D. 345 and 420. Jerome revised the various Latin translations of the Scriptures which were current in his time. In those old Latin versions Jerome found our original Greek word translated by *cotidianum*, the Latin word for "daily"; and he used that in Luke's version of the Lord's prayer. But Jerome was obviously unhappy about that meaning because in Matthew's version of the Lord's Prayer he used another Latin word *supersubstantialis*, a word that means "above all the substance". If we follow that line of reasoning then what we are praying for is not ordinary bread, but the bread which is Christ's body, the bread we receive at the altar.

There are, of course, other suggestions as to what our original Greek word meant. Some scholars – and they are perhaps the majority today – hold that it means something like "next, coming, following, future", others say that it means "present, existing", or "necessary".

There are, therefore, two main ways of interpreting "give us this day our daily bread". One way is to understand the bread as earthly bread: the other way gives it the spiritual sense of the bread of heaven – there is simply no way of knowing which way is the right way. Thus, at the very heart of the Lord's Prayer, and in what appears to be its simplest petition, there is uncertainty. Perhaps it's a warning to us not to be too dogmatic about this or that detail in the faith or indeed in faith in general whether Christian or non-Christian - certainly, there have been many casualties as a result of an excess of zeal.

The Book of Psalms may suggest another helpful way to understand our word. Psalm 30:8 says, "*give me neither poverty nor riches: feed me with the food that is needful for me*". That way, what we are praying for in the Lord's Prayer is for sufficient bread, bread that we need, neither more nor less, for just enough to get along with for the time being. That interpretation is a solitary rebuke about greed and rampant appetites.

The fact that there is so much uncertainty over the word translated "daily", and so many suggestions possible as to what it means should not alarm us. As we use the prayer every day, and perhaps more than once in a day, we can profitably move from one to another of all the meanings suggested – to do so will certainly help us on our way back to God. Bear in mind as you use the prayer also these following three points:

Firstly, the petition shows how entirely and completely we depend upon God, for both our material needs and our spiritual needs.

Secondly, it is a prayer for "efficiency" not for luxury: and so it condemns the greed and avarice and cupidity so characteristic of society today.

Thirdly, it asks for "our" bread, not "my" bread – we are praying not so much for the needs of the individual but for the needs of the community – again, a very necessary correction to the overweening individualism that ruins so much of life today.

And forgive us our trespasses, as we forgive those who trespass against us

"And forgive us our trespasses". A difference in wording here between Matthew and Luke. Matthew says, "and forgive us our debts as we have forgiven our debtors". Luke says, "and forgive us our sins, for we ourselves forgive everyone indebted to us". The difference doesn't matter, however: Luke makes it clear that "sin" and "debt" mean the same.

God forgiving sins did not originate in Christianity. There are prayers for forgiveness in Syrian and Egyptian cults and in the ancient Greek world generally. The Old Testament is emphatic on the subject of divine forgiveness. Exodus says that "*God [is] merciful and gracious, longsuffering, and abundant in goodness and truth: keeping mercy for thousands, forgiving iniquity and transgression and sin*".[80] The Psalms are always going on about sins before being forgiven. Before Jesus came on the scene the goal and purpose of John Baptist's mission was forgiveness of sins.

The message of forgiveness of sins may not have originated with Jesus but Jesus was more than emphatic about the need for forgiveness. There's Peter's famous question in Matthew, "*Lord, how often shall my brother sin against me, and I forgive him? As many as seven times?*" Jesus said to him, "*Not seven times seven but, I tell you, seventy-seven times seven*".[81] Luke has the story of the woman who sinned but much was forgiven her because she loved much. Then there's the poignant and heart-breaking

---

80 Exodus 34:6

81 Matthew 18:21

cry from the cross, *"Father, forgive them for they do not know what they do"*.[82]

What is new in Christianity is that our sins can be forgiven because God sent his Son into the world for precisely that purpose. Remember how Jesus explained the reason why he healed the paralytic. He told the Scribes that he had done it so that they might know that the Son of Man has power on earth to forgive sins. Remember also what he said to the paralytic himself, *"Your sins are forgiven you"*.[83] Our belief that Jesus came into the world to forgive sins is summed up at the very beginning of Matthew's gospel – *"he shall save his people from their sins"*.[84]

Two things are absolutely essential for the Christian: a sense of total dependence upon God and a sense of sin. Paul, in his letter to the Romans, was emphatic about the second – *"all have sinned,"* he roundly declared, *"and fall short of the glory of God"*.[85] If we do not have a genuine sense of our sinfulness then we have no real desire for forgiveness. We can only say this part of the Lord's Prayer sincerely as penitents, not only aware of our sins but really and truly sorry for them. We must realise also that we ourselves cannot put right what has gone wrong – only God can do so. The initiative as always has to come from God, and the initiative came, of course, in the person of Jesus our blessed Lord and Saviour.

"As we forgive those who trespass against us". What does that mean? Do we have to forgive others before God will forgive us? Or do we forgive others because God has forgiven us? We can answer those questions only when we have really and truly got hold of the Christian message. When we sin, we cut ourselves off from the community of love: when we sin, we separate ourselves from the love of God. When we are filled with hate and refuse to forgive, we

---

82 Luke 23:34

83 Mark 2:5

84 Matthew 1:21

85 Romans 3:23

cannot accept God's offer of love. When we forgive, we can really only do so because we know that God loves us and wants to make everything right with us and with everybody else.

Lead us not into temptation

"And lead us not into temptation." Not an easy request to understand. In fact, St James, in his letter, seems to contradict the Lord's Prayer. James says, "*Let no one say when they are tempted, "I am being tempted by God"* ... *God himself tempts no one. But each person is tempted when he is lured and enticed by his own desire.*"[86]

Earlier in his letter, however, James had said something rather different, "*Count it all joy, my brothers and sisters, when you fall into manifold temptations.*"[87] Perhaps we ought to ask therefore, exactly why we should pray not to be led into temptation.

Temptation is an inescapable part of the Bible story. The whole Bible may be said to be the book of temptations from beginning to end, from the temptation in the Garden of Eden where Adam and Eve sinned, to the garden of Gethsemane where Our Lord himself was tempted.

Perhaps we ought to say that temptation is not in itself a thing to welcome and that we should always try to avoid it. We have, therefore, after all, Our Lord's example: in the garden of Gethsemane, knowing that he was to suffer, he prayed, "*Father, if it is Your will, take this cup away from Me; nevertheless not My will, but Yours, be done*".[88]

It is, of course, the end bit of that prayer that tells us such a lot. Our Lord knew that he was going to suffer, he did not want to suffer, yet he was prepared to accept whatever God wanted. We do not always know the end of the story: we have to trust God all the way through.

---

[86] James 1:13
[87] James 1:2
[88] Luke 22:42

The actual Greek word for temptation, *teiprasmos*, doesn't just mean temptation to sin. It includes every kind of test or trial. For the early Christians it often meant the persecutions that fell upon the infant Church. Any test or trial we suffer brings with it the possibility of our falling by the wayside and believing no longer. It is so easy to blame God when things go wrong but that's what Our Lord didn't do in the garden of Gethsemane.

The bishop[89] who made me both deacon and priest had this to say about temptation. He pointed out that in Gethsemane Jesus turned to his disciples and said, "*Pray that you may not enter into temptation.*"[90] As the bishop pointed out, the disciples were going right into the sharpest temptations they had yet experienced – the temptation to run away (as they all did), to retaliate (as one of them did), or even to deny Jesus altogether (as Peter did). But that does not mean, said the bishop, that they did not say their prayers, or that their prayers were not answered – the temptation was not that they should fail but that they shouldn't care whether they failed or not. The real temptation in life is to lose interest, to allow our vision to become clouded and murky, to see good as evil, and evil as good. It is against that temptation that we must always pray to be delivered.

But deliver us from evil

The last petition in the Lord's prayer has also caused a great deal of controversy. The word "but" links it closely with the preceding petition, and many people take it to be an interpretation or explanation of that petition, "lead us not into temptation". Some have argued, however, that it does not really add anything and is not really necessary. Certainly, Luke does not include it in his version of the prayer, and perhaps it was added to Matthew's version later on. On the other hand, we must remember that the first

---

[89] John Moorman, Bishop of Ripon 1959-1975. Dad was deaconed in 1962 and priested in 1963

[90] Luke 22:46

Christians were Jews before they became Christian; and later Judaism concentrated on one great enemy or tempter or evil one: so it's not really surprisingly that the New Testament also mentioned evil.

Again, not surprisingly, the Old Testament has many parallels to the petition. Genesis describes God as "*the angel who hath redeemed me from all evil*".[91] Psalm 17:13 says "*deliver my soul from the wicked*" that is from the wicked one; and the Psalter as a whole contains more than one similar saying. Proverbs says, "*discretion will watch over you, understanding will guard you*".[92] Wisdom says, "*thou art he who deliverest from all evil*".[93] The New Testament contains several references to the wicked or to evil outside of the Lord's Prayer. For example, "*I pray... but you should keep them from the evil one*",[94] or, "*the Lord shall deliver me from every evil work*".[95]

Those quotations also suggest how we might interpret the original Greek word for evil in the phrase "deliver us from evil". There are three main possibilities:

Firstly, the Greek original may be referring to evil man. In fact, no scholar accepts that interpretation – it's too narrow an interpretation.

Secondly, the Greek original may simply mean evil in general. That's what St Augustine, for example, thought, and the whole of the Western or Latin Church accepts that view.

Thirdly, the Greek original may mean the evil one or the devil. That is the view of the Eastern Orthodox Church; and in fact various passages in the New Testament support that interpretation.

Whether we take the Western view that it refers to evil in general or whether we take the Eastern view that it refers to the devil, the words of the petition take us back to the beginning of the prayer. The prayer began by concentrating

---

91 Genesis 48:16
92 Proverbs 2:11
93 Wisdom 16:8
94 John 17:15
95 2 Timothy 4:18

our attention upon the Father and his power – "Our Father who art in heaven". The final petition reminds us how helpless we are when faced with evil in any form – we have no power in ourselves to help ourselves: we have to be snatched out of danger by a power from on high. "Snatched" is a really strong word and does far better justice to the force of the Greek word translated "deliver".

The phrase reminds us also that there is the power of deliverance: we are not in this dangerous world on our own. We may be subject to temptation but if we believe in God we can look to him, our shield and protector, for rescue – and we can look to him with the utmost confidence because he is our Father in heaven.

The prayer ends as it began, by fixing our attention firmly upon God – there is, after all, no other name by which we shall be saved.

"Deliver us from evil" is in fact, the last sentence of the Lord's Prayer. It brings the prayer to an end in all the manuscripts of Luke's version. Only later manuscripts for Matthew's gospel add what is called the doxology "for thine is the kingdom, the power and the glory".

It's not surprisingly that the doxology was added – its words are very ancient: they were brought together from various parts of the Jewish liturgy. The doxology may be said to be older than Christianity, therefore, and it reminds us of our Jewish heritage, the firm belief in one God, and one God only. The doxology is a most suitable outburst of praise with which to end our great Christian family prayer. We are not Christians, we cannot be the Christian family unless and until we put God at the very centre of all our living, God and nobody else, God and nothing else.

Ensuring that we do put God at the centre and the heart of our existence is not easy. One way of doing so is to really pray the Lord's Prayer, to say the Lord's Prayer not just with our lips, but with our mind, our hearts, all our powers of reflection and loving. Here St Ignatius of Loyola has a good piece of advice to offer. Ignatius recommended saying one word of a prayer at a time, at the top of each breath, holding the breath just long enough to say the word – that should enable us really to mark, learn, and inwardly digest what we are praying, whether it is the Lord's Prayer or any other prayer in fact.

We have now looked in detail at each of the petitions of the Lord's Prayer to tease out the meaning of each. But the best next step will come in the days and weeks and months and years ahead as we pray the Lord's Prayer with an increasing devotion, understanding, and with more and more of our living shaped and formed by it.

Questions for discussion or reflection

- *Have you ever paused to consider the meaning of each petition of the Lord's Prayer?*
- *Were you surprised that not all the petitions in the prayer are straightforward to understand? If so, which surprised you the most and why?*
- *Bearing in mind what you have learnt from the chapter looking at how to pray, how will you pray the Lord's Prayer going forward?*

The sacraments of baptism, confirmation, marriage and the Eucharist

The Church has seven sacraments: baptism, confirmation, the Eucharist, confession and absolution, holy matrimony, ordination and unction (or the anointing of the sick). Not all Christians receive or take part in all of the sacraments, for example not everyone is called to holy matrimony or to take holy orders and be ordained. This chapter reminds us what the sacraments of baptism, confirmation, holy matrimony and the Eucharist entail.

Baptism

Baptism – the only way to become a Christian

When I was a vicar myself, I always administered baptism at a time when, to quote the words of the Book of Common Prayer, "the most number of people come together". These days that happens at the Holy Communion. Indeed, the vicar of the parish where we worshipped when my daughters were born allowed me to baptise each of them during the main Sunday service.

Some people do not like Holy Baptism to take place during a Holy Communion. Perhaps they do not realise that Holy Baptism is a more important sacrament than Holy Communion. There are, of course, other ways of communion with God than Holy Communion, though they are certainly not as essential. But there is only one way of becoming a Christian, and that is through Holy Baptism.

Holy Communion is the form of worship peculiar to the Christian Church. It is vital, therefore, for the fellowship of the members of the Church that they attend Holy Communion regularly. But Holy Baptism makes a most important distinction. In Holy Baptism we turn from the self-centredness of our animal nature, to the self-sacrifice which is of God. In Holy Baptism we renounce the attitude and outlook of the non-baptised members of mankind, however moral and sincere those members may be. From Holy Baptism onwards we are to walk with God and not follow the ways of the world.

Holy Baptism is of the utmost importance, therefore. Except in an emergency, it must never take place privately but always in public. At times when, to repeat the phrase, the most number of the people come together. In addition, we must not even think of the administration of Holy Baptism as being in any way incidental to something else. When Holy Baptism takes place during the Holy Communion, we must not think of it as merely a starter as it were to our Holy Communion. We should think of our Holy Communion as being enriched, enhanced, by the fact that it is taking place at the time of Holy Baptism, when a new person is received into the body of Christ.

One of the things that put Andrea, my wife, off me at our first meeting was that I did not approve of infant baptism. I still think there is a great deal to be said, though not everything, for postponing baptism to the time of confirmation. Both parts of the sacrament can then be administered to candidates who themselves desire it. What makes infant baptism a reality is the desire of the parents and godparents on behalf of the child they love. There is nothing strange or improper about that. Wise parents give their children many things and much advice before the children understand or appreciate what they are doing. The parents do so because they believe, and hope, that their children will live to thank them for doing so. That is why I baptised our infant daughters when they were infants.

We call the sacraments outward and visible signs. They are outward and visible signs of an intention. That intention isn't the intention of one moment in time only – it is an intention for life. The outward and visible sign of the sacrament is not, therefore, a material object, which we can locate in a particular place or moment. So, it is not the water of baptism, nor the bread and wine of Holy Communion, that are the outward signs – it's the action. After all, there's nothing particularly significant in a kiss, but there is a great deal of significance in the giving of a kiss. It is not the kiss itself but the giving of it in a particular way that signifies love – there is all the difference in the world between the kiss of a Judas and the kiss of those people who love.

Thus, the outward sign of the sacraments, the means by which we receive the inward and spiritual grace, are: the immersion in water and the strengthening of a touch in baptism or confirmation, and the setting aside and receiving of bread and wine in Holy Communion.

The outward sign of being immersed in water and rising-up refreshed symbolises forgiveness. When we forgive, or are forgiven, two things happen simultaneously, two quite distinct things which are nevertheless inseparable. There is the freedom from the awful burden of our past conduct, and the freedom for a different and better life in the future. That is what the outward sign of baptism and confirmation is, the sign of being freed from the chains and fetters of our animal life, with its selfishness without which we could not survive in this world. At the same time, it is the sign of receiving the life of true unselfishness, that life which alone can really satisfy us but which we cannot receive except from God.

At whatever age we are baptised there is no reason why we should not be confirmed at the same time. That is what happens in some parts of Christendom. We in this country find a practical value in separating baptism and confirmation. We want children to grow in the Christian family before they commit themselves to the duties and privileges their parents wanted for them at their baptism. But if we allow baptism to be just a ceremony, something done and finished with at a particular moment in time, then baptism is of little use or value, especially when the baptised receive no further help.

That further help is, of course, the primary responsibility of the parents and godparents of the baptised. But it must also be a concern of the whole Church. Infant baptism may be useless and of little value, not just because of the parents and godparents but also because of the people in the parishes in which the children live. I have lived and worked in several different parts of the country, and I know how little is done for many children who have been baptised in infancy. They need to have a living interest taken in them as they try to grow in the fellowship of the Church. It is not easy but we must not be content to leave it there. We have to show all those whom we receive by Holy Baptism that we are their friends, and that our fellowship with God is something which it is worthwhile for them to enjoy.

What sort of organisation do the baptised become members of?

When someone is baptised, they are admitted into the fellowship of Christ's church. What sort of organisation is it that we are going to make a newly baptised person a member of?

There is more than one definition or description of the Church. The suffering community; the people of God; the worshipping community; the witnessing community – those are some of the soundbites that are used to describe the Church.

St Paul had a far better definition of the Church. He described it as the body of Christ. That description needs some explaining.

You and I are made up of three parts: body, mind and spirit. In this life here on earth we can express ourselves only through the body. Our mind and our spirit may be vigorous and active but they both need the body to convey our thoughts and our feelings. St Paul is saying, therefore, that our minds and our spirits need our bodies to express themselves; and in the same way Christ expresses himself here on earth through his body, the Church.

That is probably the most important fact for us Christians to grasp. The Church is not just a convenient way of gathering into one all the would-be followers of Christ. The Church is something that exists in itself. It is something we need to join before we can call ourselves Christians. The

Church is something that exists whether you or I decide to join it or not.

The only parallel is that of the family. The family, any family, is composed of its various members. At the same time, you and I and everybody else are members of a family because the family gives us life. It is the age-old question of which comes first – "the hen or the egg?" - the problem of the one and the many. An earthly family can speak and act only through its members. Similarly, we who are Christians are Christ's body in the world. We Christians are now Christ's mouth, Christ's eyes, his tongue, his hands and his feet. Christ carries on his activities in the world of today through us.

Christ cannot now go anywhere in the world as a missionary except through those of his followers who call themselves Christians. Christ cannot carry out an Act of Parliament except through those of his followers who have been elected MPs. Christ cannot make roads or houses, run charitable organisations, work in hospitals or schools, except in the persons of his followers who are engaged in those activities. The Church is the body of Christ: we are members or limbs of that body – it is our job to do Christ's will in the world. That, of course, gives rise to a very practical question. What exactly is our job as members of the Church? What is the Christian's task? What is a Christian for?

The answer to that question lies in two words already mentioned: worship and witness. Not to make us good; not primarily to do anything for us at all – a great Archbishop of Canterbury, William Temple[96], once said famously, that the Church is the only organisation that exists for the benefit of those outside it. The Church exists to do something for God and for the world; and that something we sum up in the two words, "worship" and "witness".

Worship is getting to know God, giving God his due worth. Witness is telling other people what we have found

---

[96] William Temple was Archbishop of Canterbury 1942-1944.

out about God, telling them what God's due worth is. And the interesting fact is that we cannot satisfactorily engage in either of those two activities if we are not doing them both equally. We cannot witness unless we are already worshipping; and our worship is not worth anything if we do not witness.

Being a Christian is not, therefore, a solitary activity: being a Christian is not something we can be by ourselves. Christianity is a way of life; as such it involves other people. The Christian virtues are not worth having if we do not put them into practice among other people. We cannot possibly acquire the Christian virtues if we do not join with other Christians in regular worship.

Worship and witness are the two essential and defining characteristics of the Christian life. They mean that it is no good calling ourselves members of the Church if we rarely go to church. They mean also that it is no good just being moral and upright people. There are many moral and upright people outside the Church; in fact, some people outside the Church can be better people than some inside it.

Our worship is not therefore genuine unless we also witness, and our witness cannot be effective if we are not worshipping. Of course, witnessing means more than talking. We witness most effectively by our lives, by things we do and the things we do not do. Being true members of the Church, not just being seen to go to church but being seen as people to whom church-going makes all the difference in their lives – that is how witness works best of all.

Worship and witness, the two essential characteristics of the Christian life. And something else is also needed: faithfulness. "Be thou faithful" as a hymn by an anonymous author says. We must strive, regularly and quietly worshipping and witnessing, doing our Christian duty, that is, and leaving the rest to God. If we have sufficient trust in God to know that he is alive and active on earth still, through his body the Church, then miracles will happen, providing we play our part and faithfully carry on Christ's work,

134

worshipping and witnessing; just being in our place, giving God his due worth and showing others with our kiss and in our lives what his due worth is. We may not see the results for ourselves in our lifetime but let us be always confident that what we do as Christians will never be in vain.

Psalm 23 – a psalm for baptism

Psalm 23 is a very popular psalm. We sing it at weddings and at funerals. In the version known as Crimond many people ask for it who would not describe themselves as being very religious at all.

What many people do not realise is that Psalm 23 is suitable and appropriate not just for weddings and funerals but it is also very much a psalm for baptism. Throughout Christendom, Psalm 23 has, in fact, been linked with baptism and for a very long time.

Look at the stained glass in many a Victorian church and you will often see the pictures and imagery of Psalm 23 linked with baptism, especially the image of the Good Shepherd. Far away from Victorian England, in the Syrian desert, in the ancient city of Dura Europos, in a house built there in the 3rd century, a painting of the Good Shepherd is to be seen close by the font.

Victorian times are not so far distant from us; but Dura Europos is both an old city and very far away. It lies on the right-hand side of the River Euphrates between the cities of Aleppo and Baghdad. In Dura Europos there has been found the earliest known Christian church, circa A.D. 232. The church was made from two rooms in a private house - the dividing walls between the two rooms having been taken down. A third room was converted for use as a baptistery, and there beside the font was discovered the painting of the Good Shepherd. I've already mentioned the linking of Psalm 23 with baptism is both worldwide and constant throughout time, therefore.

"*The Lord is my Shepherd*". Actually, Psalm 23 does not begin exactly like that in the Hebrew, its original language. Here, as so often, we come up against the problem of translation, of how to convey in a foreign language what was originally said in another language.

Psalm 23 really speaks of "our shepherding Lord". The form of that word "shepherding" tells us that God is always on the look-out for our welfare and that, like any good shepherd, he is always guiding and turning us into the way we should go. How appropriate Psalm 23 is for baptism: for what is baptism but the beginning of our Christian journey, a journey on which we are to follow Christ's lead.

"He makes me lie down in green pastures. He leads me beside quiet waters". Psalm 23 was written for nomads, for people who wandered about the countryside to find fresh pastures for their animals because the old pastures had been over-grazed, and because the water-courses changed with the seasons. If the sheep were allowed to remain in the same place all the time they would die for lack of pasture.

Similarly, we Christians cannot remain the same forever. We are to grow into the fullness of the stature of Christ; and that means constantly leaving our own wicked and immoral selves behind as we journey onwards towards Christ's promises of life, and life abundant.

"He guides me in paths of righteousness for his name's sake". As he wrote those words the psalmist had a certain picture in mind, the picture of a liturgical procession led by an anointed sovereign or ruler who was carrying rod and staff - orb and sceptre - that is the symbols of God's authority. Psalm 23 is very much a baptismal psalm, therefore, because baptism joins us to that royal procession which Christ leads and which we are to walk with Christ all the days of our life.

When I baptised a baby in the East Yorkshire village of Seaton Ross, I noticed that the font in the church there, though a lovely stone one, is fairly plain without much decoration on it. When fonts do have decoration upon them, we usually see somewhere doves feeding from the vine. The vine represents the heavenly banquet or feast we celebrate with God. We celebrate that feast intermittently here on earth, whenever we come to the Holy Communion, and we know that the Holy Communion is but a foretaste of the splendid feast we shall enjoy in heaven with God, the holy angels, and all the saints who have gone before.

The table or altar is ready and waiting for us; and at it we shall receive our Holy Communion, the body and the blood of our dear Lord himself, the finest food of all. It is now that Psalm 23 gives us a solemn warning – *"you prepare a table before me in the presence of my enemies"*. That is why King David is said to have prayed this psalm as he was taking refuge from his enemies in the wilderness; and we Christians have many enemies in the world, enemies who mock our Lord and think little of the good work we try to do here on earth.

I mentioned earlier the problem of translation. The Latin version of Psalm 23 has an interesting insight here. It renders "before me" by *contra me*, "against me" implying that the feast God sets before us not only refreshes but also confronts our doubts, our sins, our fears – which one of us has not sometimes prayed, "Lord let me believe, but not just yet?" It can be very hard to walk the way of Christ; we may be looking forward to the heavenly feast but it is so easy to fall by the wayside. We should use the words of Psalm 23 to reflect upon our journey with Christ.

Confirmation and first communion

First communion is a very special occasion. It is one of the great days in the life of the Church. For at a service of Holy Communion we welcome our newly confirmed members of the Catholic Church. Some come to be confirmed having been baptised as adults, others were baptised as children or babies. It does not matter when their baptism took place. Their baptism was their first great step into the Church. When they were confirmed by the Bishop, that was their second great step into the Church. Now they have made their way to the Eucharist to make their first Communion, and so become full members of the Holy Catholic and Apostolic Church.

It is surely a great joy to all of us to see them taking part for the first time in the full worship of Almighty God. They will no doubt be feeling rather nervous and not quite at their ease as they prepare to make their way to the altar there to receive the holy bread and wine. Let us therefore who are already members of the Church, who have grown to know and to love the ways of our Church so well, let us do our best during the weeks and months ahead to make these new members of the Church feel more and more at ease in their Father's house and at their Father's service. Let us support them with our love and friendship and prayers as they, like us, tread the path of obedience to God, which is so often such a hard and stony road. Let us look for them at the altar week by week as they try to let Jesus come even closer to them and let us miss them when they are not there.

It is often said, and too often it is true, that youth and age do not go well together. I have spoken of our attitude towards young people who come to first communion but what of their attitude towards us? What will their reaction be to us? Will they, do they, see in us the faithful regular members of the Church which we hope and pray they will become? We, like them, are equally people under orders. We like them were once baptised and the priest signed our forehead with a sign of the cross, thereby showing that we had enlisted in the Christian army, that we had become soldiers of Christ.

Now the very essence of a soldier is that the soldier is a person under authority, that the soldier can never do as he or she likes but must obey the orders given him or her. The soldier is not a true soldier who does not obey orders. And so, for us who are Christians, whether recently become so or made so long ago – it does not matter, for all of us the question is not so much, why? why must I do this or that? But rather, is there an order? Because if there is an order, we, the soldiers in the Christian army, are under obligation to obey and carry it out.

Now there is one order which our captain has given us. It was on the Thursday night, the very night that he was caught and made prisoner. It was, we might say, his dying act, as on the next day he was nailed to the cross. But when the night before he had gathered his small band of apostles together and in a little upper room, he began by saying: with desire I have desired to eat this Passover with you. Put into English, that means: I have been looking forward to this meeting for some time, more than I can say. Let us think about that. It was his last act, his dying act, and he said that he had been looking forward to it. Quite clearly, he wanted his disciples to understand that something quite extraordinary was about to take place.

He then took the bread and blessed it saying: this is my body. He then took the cup with some wine and said this is my blood, and immediately afterwards he turned to his apostles and said: do this – this very thing that I am doing – do this in remembrance of me – do it to show that you have not forgotten me. That is most certainly an order, without a shadow of a doubt, Jesus' dying order. If my father on his death-bed gave me an order I should consider that such an order solemnly binding on me. Nor had the disciples any doubts that it was an order too, because as we read the early chapters of Acts of the Apostles, a book which tells us what the first Christians were accustomed to do, we come across this or some such similar phrase again and again, that they met for prayer and the breaking of the bread, which is of course only another name for the Eucharist.

But the glory of our captain is that he never gives an order simply for the sake of giving us something to do. Perhaps all our life through, there are some people who are always on at us to do something. Just in order to keep us busy and therefore, they hope, out of mischief. But the Lord Jesus Christ is not at all like that. When he gives an order there is always a very good reason for it; and he has given us an excellent reason why we should never fail to come to the Eucharist, even if we go to church only once on a Sunday. He took the bread and blessed it and said, this is my body; he took the cup with the wine in it and said, this is my blood.

Now, you will find many people who try to explain those words away so that they do not mean anything like what they sound. Some will say that the bread is no longer bread and the wine is no longer wine. Some will say that the bread remains just bread and the wine just wine and nothing more. The Church of England explains it in this way. It is true that the bread still looks like bread and tastes like bread. It is true that the wine still looks like wine and tastes like wine. We cannot explain it and we do not understand it, but we can take the Lord at his word, and every time those words are spoken, he is there, very God and very human in his own special way – our King and captain has come into our midst in a very near and special moment, hidden from our sight in the bread and wine.

We see now why Jesus orders us to be here in church at such a time. If our captain is holding a review of his soldiers, he will expect us to be present, to pay him homage, shout hallelujah, God save the King. That is why the finest music in the world has been written round the service of Holy Communion. That is why we priests wear special clothes at this time which we never wear at any other time. That is why we burn candles. That is why we decorate the church with flowers because we say – the King is coming to hold his review and we do not want him to come to a room all bare and ugly but to a building made as beautiful and lovely as we can make it.

Every Sunday our church bells ring out to tell us that King Jesus is coming to hold his review, and I must be there and you must be there to shout God save the King, hallelujah. Two thousand years ago the Lord Jesus Christ came into our midst as a little baby in a manger, and many people could not believe that God would come to his people in such a simple, humble way. Today he comes in the form of bread and wine. In this way he holds his review week by week, and he looks for us. What a great sorrow he must feel when we, his soldiers are not loyal enough to come to pray. From now on to our dying day, unless we are sick or prevented by causes we cannot alter we must be here every

Sunday. Even when we are on holiday, we must not on that account to be absent from the Eucharist because the King will still be holding his review at the church in the place where we are and we as true loyal soldiers must be there, always there, in obedience and homage to do this in remembrance of him who did everything for us.

Marriage

The start of the wedding service reminds us that Christ attended a wedding. At that wedding Christ was concerned for his friends, the bride and her groom. Their arrangements had gone wrong – the wine was running out. Christ did not want their wedding to be spoilt: he supplied more wine, therefore, very good wine, which improved the party atmosphere no end.

Some people are surprised that Christ attended a wedding – they think of him as a killjoy, not a party-goer, enjoying himself in company. Such people have forgotten that Christ himself said that he came to bring us life, abundant life. In other words, Christ is a life-enhancer. Thus he always strongly emphasised loving God and loving our neighbour. Christ wants us to do what is right, not out of a sense of duty, but for the love of God and our neighbour.

The wedding Christ attended was a suitable occasion for him to perform his first miracle or sign. A true marriage is a favour from God, a foretaste of the joys of heaven. When couples come to be married, they know what they want to do in being married. What they are doing is the will of God. As they care for one another, the bride and groom are caring for the will of God.

Not all weddings are wonderful, however. There are, sadly, selfish couples, partners out only for what he or she can get from the other. Such selfish couples do not have a Christian marriage. In Christian marriage God brings two people together to join him in the work of creation. Through two people married to one another, God creates a newly shared existence, a newly founded home, a new family, a new life-cell in the body of Christ.

The wedding Christ attended shows the way to a sound marriage relationship. Christ's mother told him that the wine was running out. Christ asked what that had to do with him. Christ's mother did not argue back – she simply turned to the wine-stewards and said: "do whatever he tells you". Christ and his mother – two people with different principles but deciding whose principles were better on a particular occasion – a good rule for good living.

Christian people, in truly caring for one another in marriage, are caring for the will of God. If we care for God and for one another, we taste the wine of happiness at the start of our married lives, and as our relationships deepen, strengthen, and change – and change for the better they do, if we work hard at them – then we shall taste the wine of ever-increasing happiness until, as Christ promised, we drink it with him in paradise.

Eucharist

The jewel that is the Eucharist

Corpus Christi Day. Body of Christ Day. The day when we thank God for the Holy Eucharist. I still remember vividly the Sunday after Corpus Christi Day in my first year at Oxford. I'd just started to take an active interest in the Christian religion. The low church or evangelically minded members of my college thought they had me as one of them. I was going to so many of their Bible study groups and prayer meetings.

A friend then decided to broaden my experience of church life: he took me to a solemn high Mass. What an experience! The then assistant Bishop of Oxford was the celebrant; he wore all the vestments of a Bishop at the altar. From the pulpit, the Bishop preached a forceful evangelistic sermon. Another highlight of the service was the procession of the Blessed Sacrament around the church: the Bishop held consecrated bread up high; before him little girls in white dresses scattered rose petals on the floor: clouds of sweet smelling incense swirled upwards: and we all sang heartily.

Following that, the members of the evangelical group in college knocked on my door. In they came and arranged themselves in a semicircle around me. They rebuked me for going to that particular church and warned me that if I continued to go to services like that one, I would probably end up in the arms of "the scarlet woman", the Church of Rome. They foresaw no worse a fate for me.

That did it. Ever since then I have been happiest with the service that includes music, bells, and incense. However, almost as soon as those college members left my room, I made two vows: I would never talk down to those who want the Eucharist celebrated differently from me: and I would always observe the way of celebrating usual in any church to which I might be invited. More than once I have stood at the north end of the altar, wearing cassock, black scarf, and hood of my university degree. Ever since that far off day in Oxford I have tried to walk in the way of tolerance and acceptance of diversity that has long been characteristic of the Church of England but is not so now.

Of all the services the Church has to offer, the Eucharist is the greatest jewel. The Book of Common Prayer tells us how important the Eucharist is when it provides a collect, epistle and gospel for every Sunday, the great festivals of Christmas, Easter, Pentecost and the Ascension, and for certain Saints' days also. Common Worship goes even further than the Book of Common Prayer: it provides readings for every day of the week. I was fortunate that one of my Norfolk parishes wanted a celebration of the Eucharist every day. On any one day there may have been only two or three gathered together, but Christ's sacrifice was duly proclaimed. Not without reason is the Eucharist described as "the beating heart" of the Church. In the Eucharist the whole Christ is present, the Christ of Bethlehem, Calvary, Easter, the Ascension. Jesus of Nazareth, Son of God and Son of Mary, is present in the world in the Eucharist, is surely present only through the Eucharist.

Dom Gregory Dix was a member of our only Anglican Benedictine community of monks. He wrote a book entitled,

"The shape of the Liturgy".[97] That book had an enormous influence in the early stages of political revision and renewal in the Anglican Church. It is also a book which is beautifully written. One of its most magnificent passages comes when Dix asks if even another command has been obeyed as much as our Lord's command, "do this in remembrance of me"....

"Was ever another command so obeyed? For century after century, spreading slowly to every continent and country and among every race of earth, this action has been done, in every conceivable human circumstance, for every conceivable human need, for infancy and before it to extreme old age and after it, from the pinnacles of earthly greatness to the refuge of fugitives in the caves and dens of the earth. Men have found no better thing than this to do for Kings at their crowning and for criminals going to the scaffold; for armies in triumph or for a bride and bridegroom in a little country church; for the proclamation of a dogma, or for a good crop of wheat; for the wisdom of the Parliament of a mighty nation or for a sick old woman afraid to die; for a schoolboy sitting an examination or for Columbus setting out to discover America; for the famine of whole provinces or for the soul of the dead lover; in thankfulness because my father did not die of pneumonia; for the village Headman much tempted to return to fetish because the yams had failed; because the Turk was at the gates of Vienna; for the repentance of Margaret; for the settlement of a strike; for the son of a barren woman; for Captain so-and-so, wounded and prisoner of war; while the lions roared in the nearby amphitheatre; on the beach at Dunkirk; while the hiss of scythes in the thick June grass came faintly through the windows of the church; tremulously, by an old monk on the 50th anniversary of his vows; furtively, by an exiled bishop who had hewn timber all day in a prison camp in Murmansk; gloriously, for the canonisation of St Joan of Arc - one could fill many pages

---

[97] Extract from The Shape of the Liturgy by Dom Gregory Dix

with the reasons why men have done this, and not tell 100th part of them. And best of all, week by week and month by month, on 100,000 successive Sundays, faithfully, unfailingly, across all the parishes of Christendom, the pastors have done this just to *make* the *plebs sancta Deii* - the holy common people of God."

The three movements of the Eucharist

I was trained as a priest in the parish of Adel in the northern suburbs of Leeds. I felt that I had made a wise decision when I accepted the Rector's offer for me to go there. I was even more certain when I made my first Communion there. It was at a sung Eucharist and immediately after the prayer of consecration we sang hymn number 416 from Hymns Ancient and Modern revised: –

Wherefore, o Father, we thy humble servants
Here bring before the Christ thy well beloved
All perfect offering, sacrifice immortal,
Spotless oblation.

After more than 40 years I still like to sing that hymn. For me it puts the emphasis on the Communion Service exactly where it should be. Like many other people I sometimes fall into the habit of thinking that the only reason for the Holy Communion is that *I* may make my communion. Hymn 416 tells me, however, that the first purpose of the Holy Communion is that in it *we* offer worship to God the Father through God the Son. We offer, we represent, Christ's sacrifice on the cross, not primarily for our education or benefit, but to the greater glory of Almighty God.

There are several movements as it were in the service of Holy Communion. One of them is the movement from God to man. That movement comes when we receive God into ourselves at the altar rails. But we must never forget the movement that comes first, the movement that comes from us.

We can best explain that movement by looking at what exactly happens during the service of Holy Communion. The celebrant takes bread and wine, and places them on the altar. The celebrant takes bread and wine and places them there as a sign that each one of us has come to offer himself or herself, body and soul, entirely and without reservation to God.

Bread and wine are important and essential. Food and drink are necessary for life; and bread and wine are the work of our hands – they represent the living which we scratch from the earth. Bread and wine, placed upon the altar, represent hard work and toil. They signify us, each one of us, our hopes and our fears, our successes and our failures, the kind of people we are – what we are like at work and at play. There is a long and honourable tradition in the Church of saying that we are on the altar, in the form of bread and wine, we lie waiting ready to be offered to God the Father.

We cannot be offered just as we are, however, not even in the convenient form of bread and wine. We are too dirty, too stained and blackened by sin, to be allowed into the Father's presence straight away. As a matter of fact, throughout the world's long history, there has only been one offering to God worthy of the name that has been made, Christ's offering of himself upon the cross.

Fortunately for us Christ does not leave us lying there on the altar in bread and wine, lost and ruined forever in our sins and wrongdoing. Jesus takes our poor offering of ourselves and joins it to his perfect offering of himself to the Father so that, in the words of the hymn, we plead before the Father a spotless oblation, a sacrifice immortal, Christ the well beloved of the Father.

So, the first movement in the Eucharist is the movement from man to God through the Son. There then takes place the second movement as it were, the movement from God to man. For the Son takes our poor offering of ourselves in bread and wine and joins it to his perfect offering of himself – this is my body; this is my blood – and the bread and wine become the body and blood of Christ, the finest food on which anyone may feed. For, as we eat and drink, in faith with thanksgiving, we have a foretaste of heaven, and for a moment in time we share in the life of the Holy Trinity – as someone once said, the Holy Eucharist is "the thinnest point in the veil between time and eternity".

Efforts to explain how this second movement happens cause controversy. Roman Catholics use Greek philosophy to arrive at an explanation. They say that, outwardly, the consecrated bread and the consecrated wine still resemble unconsecrated bread and wine, but their substance, their underlying reality, is changed into the body and blood of Christ.

Protestant reformers, on the other hand, say that the only way Jesus is present at the service is inwardly, in our hearts and in our minds, as, eating and drinking at the communion rail, we remember what Jesus did on the cross.

Queen Elizabeth the first took an admirable middle way. Asked about Christ's presence in the sacrament, she used these words: –

T'was God the word that speak it
He took the bread and brake it;
And what the word did make it,
That I believe, and take.

After those two movements have taken place, there comes a third movement: and if it doesn't take place there is not much point to the first two. That third movement comes when we move out of church into the world at large. We go out of church, fortified and comforted by what we have eaten and drunk, the body and blood of Christ. We go, having dedicated ourselves once more to God; and that dedication brings with it an enormous responsibility and privilege, the privilege and responsibility of making God known in and to the world. The world is God's, but it doesn't acknowledge itself as God's. So, it is our task to be missionaries wherever we go: not that we have to go very far – opportunities for witnessing to God arise almost as soon as we get out of church.

Three movements in the Holy Communion: –

The movement from us to God – the offertory
The movement from God to us – the communion
The movement when we go out of church as God's agents, representatives

Those three movements are vital.

The party that is the Eucharist

Before he died, Noel Coward wrote some memorable songs. One of his less well-known songs goes like this:

I went to a wonderful party
With Bertie and Luke and Nell;
We came as we were, which was lovely,
And we left as we were, which was hell!

Noel and Bertie and Luke and Nell had gone to a party with great expectations – they were looking forward to having a wonderful time. When they arrived at the party, they found it was a dry party – there was no alcohol: so, even though they came as they were, which was lovely, they left as they were, which for them was hell!

The Holy Communion is a party. The Roman Catholics call it the Mass; Anglicans refer to it as the Lord's Supper or the Eucharist; members of the Orthodox Church speak of it as the Holy Mysteries. Whatever the name we give it, this service is a party, a celebration, a feast, a banquet, got ready for us by Our Lord Jesus Christ. Now we come to this party just as we are, which is lovely. But unlike the people in Coward's song, we shall go away from it different because we shall have received God into our lives in the consecrated bread and in the consecrated wine, the best food and drink of all possible parties.

We leave the party of the Holy Communion different from what we were when we arrived at it, and we have to live that difference out in our everyday lives, our Monday to Saturday lives, outside the Church.

If you go into a Roman Catholic church, you will see a white light burning before a box. Sometimes the box is to be found on the altar or holy table, and it is called the tabernacle. In other churches, including Anglican churches, and Market Weighton is one of those churches, the box is fitted into the wall and we call it an aumbry. Whatever it is called, the box contains consecrated bread and wine kept there in safety ready to be taken out and given to faithful people of the Church who need God's support in an emergency.

I well remember an occasion when I was a parish priest in Norfolk. About 2:30am one Sunday morning I heard my telephone ring. It was one of the daughters of the Rural Dean. "Come quickly," she said, "daddy is dying and wants to make his communion before he goes."All I had to do was go into church, take consecrated bread and wine out of the tabernacle, drive to the Rural Dean's rectory, hear him make his brief confession, and administer to him the already consecrated bread and wine – he was so poorly there was not time to take the service in full.

If you are in a church in which you see a white light burning before a tabernacle or aumbry you will know that safe box contains consecrated bread and wine and you will probably see devout members of those churches going down on one knee or bowing in acknowledgement of Christ sacramentally present there in the consecrated bread and wine.

That custom has provoked many a stirring sermon. Some Christians dislike the very idea of Christ being considered present in some mysterious way in the consecrated bread and wine. Others have pointed out what they see as hypocrisy. Frank Western[98], for example, one time Bishop of Zanzibar, declared roundly that "it's no good reverencing

---

[98] Frank Western was the Bishop of Zanzibar from 1907 until his death in 1924.

Christ in the tabernacle if we don't acknowledge his presence in other people."

The book of Genesis makes a similar point and tells us that God created the heaven and the earth and saw that they were good.[99] Christians therefore do not just acknowledge Christ in the service of Holy Communion and in other people – Christians look for God in the whole of creation. That's why I said to somebody the other day – the Church was green long before the green movement started.

The way to God doesn't demand anything spectacular from us: his demand lies in the daily round and the common tasks. If we can't find God in our homes and in our work, if we can't find God in our daily routine, in the things we handle – in pots and pans, the office machinery, the mobile phone, the computer, it's no good looking for him anywhere else.

Benedict, the founder of western monasticism, was one of the early leaders of the Church. He was emphatic about the points just made, so emphatic that he regarded all the goods and utensils in his monastery as being as important as the sacred vessels of the holy table, the cup and the plate or the chalice and the patten. Benedict asks us, therefore, to sanctify (that is regard as holy), the present moment of time and look for God in it. Benedict is claiming that we can find God in the whole of life, if only we look for him.

We don't always look for God in the whole of life; that's why so much of life goes wrong – marriage and the family, for example: husbands or wives who don't look for God in one another but use one another simply for their own individual pleasure or gratification and use such phrases as "I must do my own thing", "I must have my own space". Without looking for God in everybody, without looking for God everywhere, we shall never find true happiness anywhere.

The Holy Communion is a sure and certain way God has of helping us to find him. Without the Holy Communion we

---

[99] Genesis 1:31

shall indeed find God difficult to find. One way of ensuring that Holy Communion does us good and helps us find God outside it is to devote more time outside the Holy Communion to a couple of activities found inside it, Bible reading and prayer. Do not let the Bible be the world's dustiest best seller in your homes!

We do not only read the Bible at the service of Holy Communion: we also pray. There are many different kinds of prayer – prayers of adoration, of penitence or sorrow, of thanksgiving, of intercession. There is also the very important prayer of contemplation which someone once described as "just looking at God and letting God look at me". The basic and fundamental point to get hold of about praying is that the more we pray the better it goes. If we pray only once a week, when we come to church, we shall not find praying easy, nor will it help us very much. To get the most out of prayer, we have to do lots of it, and by the clock, not just when we feel like it.

We have come to a wonderful party to feed and read and pray to God. We came as we were, which was lovely. We leave even better filled with God and we have to keep God's presence alive in us by frequent praying, by regular Bible reading until we come to our next communion. Those are the good habits we should be renewing so that we may lead a Christian and Godly way of life.

Questions for discussion or reflection

- *How do you continue to live out your baptismal vows?*
- *What is the difference between secular marriage and holy matrimony? In our increasingly secular age how can Christians encourage more couples to enter into holy matrimony?*
- *What meaning does the Eucharist hold for you? How do you take Christ out of church into your everyday life?*

The priestly vocation and the role of the laity

Most of us, regardless of whether or not we are church goers, are aware of the clergy in some shape or form. Some of us only come across them at a funeral or a wedding in church. Those of us who are Christians or who are exploring whether or not to enter the Christian life will have greater familiarity with the clergy. But how many of us truly understand the role the clergy has to play in the life of the Church and how that role interacts with that of the lay people? This chapter provides an explanation.

The sign and symbol of God's ownership

The thing I wear around my neck is called a dog collar. People are amused when they first hear its name. For there seems to be no connection at all between the men and women in the sacred ministry and the members of the dog world. The name has a deep significance, however, for all that it makes us laugh. The owner of a dog buys it a collar for two reasons. One is that he or she might fasten onto it a small brass plate on which are engraved his or her name and address. The collar is used, that is, to proclaim ownership of the dog. The other reason why a person buys a collar is in order to have some means by which to control the dog: when they are out together in busy streets the owner attaches a piece of leather to the collar, to keep the dog close by him or her. The collar is, therefore, a handy way of controlling the dog, of seeing that he does not run loose.

We can say very much the same about the collar the priest wears: perhaps, in fact, that is why it was given its name. First of all, the priest's collar distinguishes him or her from other people, it sets him or her apart. It is a sign that he or she is a member of the sacred ministry, one of God's special representatives. Like the collar the dog wears, which shows that he is not his own responsibility but his owner's, the collar which the priest wears shows that he or she is not his or her own keeper, that he or she is owned by God, has been claimed by God for a particular job. The priest's collar is, therefore, the sign and symbol of God's ownership.

We can also say this about the priest's collar, as we did about the dog's collar, that it is one of the ways God has of controlling his priests. When I am dressing in the morning, I am always conscious, as I put my collar on, that it is not the usual type of collar which people wear but that it is a part of the uniform I wear in God's service. Putting my priest's collar on is, therefore, a reminder to me that I am not my own man, at liberty to do whatever I like, but that I have given up my freedom, have surrendered my freedom of choice to God whose I am and whom I try to serve. And all through the day, whenever I become conscious of my collar, conscious that it is not like other people's collars, I am reminded whose uniform it is I am wearing. My collar is, therefore, one of the ways God has of controlling me, of keeping me in order, of seeing that I do not go outside the Christian limits.

But priests are not the only people who carry about their person a sign or symbol of God's ownership of them. Monks and nuns are distinguished from other people by the clothes they wear. When we see a monk or a nun in the street or meet one of them in a shop, their dress tells us that there is a man or a woman whose life is dedicated to God, a person on whom God has laid his finger and they have become his. And we must admit that in some way we are grateful for, we all are cheered by, that visible reminder of God still active in the life and work of dedicated men and women. In the midst of our busy lives, when we are so intent upon our own preoccupations that we rarely think about God and the claims he has on the world he has made, we are always heartened when we see the dress of a holy man or woman. It tells us that God is still there, that he has not forgotten us even if we have forgotten him.

And yet, you know, there is no need to look to the priest for a reminder about God. No need to look for a holy man or a woman to be reassured of God's care. Each one of us carries about with him or her a sign and symbol of God's ownership. It is not a sign we can see, like the priest's collar or the nun's habit, nevertheless, it is there. It was given to us after we had been washed clean with water in the font, when the priest carried us in his or her arms into the middle of the congregation and said this prayer over us, "We receive this child into the congregation of Christ's flock, and do sign him with a sign of the cross, in token that hereafter he shall not be ashamed to confess the faith of Christ crucified and manfully to fight under his banner, against sin, the world, and the devil, and to continue Christ's faithful soldier and servant unto his life's end." When the priest said the words, "and to sign him with the sign of the cross," the priest traced on our foreheads the sign of the cross, thus branding us for life as not our own but God's.

It is a pity that we can no longer see that mark of our branding. Some churches have a custom on Ash Wednesday of tracing a sign of the cross in ash on the forehead of all those who make their communion on that day and who then carry about on their person for the space of one whole day a visible reminder of that baptismal branding. But whether we observe such a custom or not – and it has much to recommend it – we all know, not one of us can escape the knowledge, that we received a mark of God's ownership at our baptism. And the memory of that branding should, as we think about it more and more, burn itself into our brain so that we never forget it. However self-willed we are, however fond of being our own keeper, however loath to surrender ourselves to God, that invisible sign of God's ownership, traced upon our forehead at our baptism, should be a perpetual reminder that we are no longer our own but God's, whose we are and who we should always be trying to serve.

Many people make use of a wooden cross or some other Christian symbol to place somewhere in the home or to display somewhere on their person. And they are very right to do so. Not only do such signs and symbols make our Christian profession known to those who we meet as we move about and to those who visit our homes, but they also serve as a reminder of our owner and of what we should be doing to please him. There is, therefore, much to be said for every Christian home having a Christian symbol placed somewhere in it and every Christian person carrying a Christian symbol somewhere about their body. But in addition to all those signs of our Christian loyalty, the best sign we can give to show that we are Christians is to shape our whole manner of life in such a way that people cannot fail to realise our Christian allegiance. Our lightest words, or simplest deeds, our innermost thoughts, all should be made as Christian as possible.

That is not a piece of pious moral exhortation. It follows from the fact of our baptism. When the priest traced Christ's symbol on our forehead, he or she branded us as Christ's people, he or she set us apart as Christ's people. For that very reason therefore, we have to behave as Christ's people, and in our attempts to do so the invisible sign of the cross marked on our forehead ought to remind us of him whose we are and who we are to serve. The Christian has nothing to do with morality in the accepted sense of the word, the Christian is not concerned first and foremost with maintaining a high standard of behaviour. His or her only desire is to serve the Master with whose sign he or she has been branded, without whose support, without whose care and love, the things of this world turn to dust and ashes. And just as the priest's collar is a badge of ownership with a reminder to him or her that his or her loyalties are not of this world, so when we are in danger of forgetting our Christian calling let us remember that invisible sign which each one of us carries on our forehead, the sign of the cross which is one and the same mark of God's ownership of us. For he bought us with a cross. The cross is also a reminder to us of the high standard expected of us, the high standard of Christ's suffering from the cross, when he gave up everything that he had and was in order to help us in obedience to his Father.

Laity are the servants of God. Clergy are the servants of the servants of God

Matthew, Mark, and Luke are what we call the synoptic gospel writers because they often used the same sources, although each in his own way. John didn't use the same sources, and so his gospel is different from the other three. However, one sentence from John's gospel summarises admirably an important lesson to be learnt from Jesus' baptism as Matthew told it, the sentence, *"Where I am, there shall also my servant be."*[100]

In order to appreciate that lesson we must again roll the film as it were of Jesus' baptism, more slowly this time so that we don't miss the details.

The scene is a crowded river-bank. People are jostling one another as they try for a better view. Some men are standing where the Jordan is shallowest. One of them seems to be helping the others to wash. But it does not seem to be much of a wash, only a quick plunge beneath the water. Now the helper seems to be having an argument with the young man who's last in the queue: they seem to be discussing who should be washing whom.

The young man has his way, and down he is helped, down beneath the waters of the river. He is supported below the surface of the water at a point lower than the rest of the people around – they look down at him beneath the water.

The young man is helped to his feet again, and at the same time there is a disturbance somewhere – thunder, or the noise of the crowd? But some people are claiming that they have actually made out certain words, words of approval of the young man, but whose words? There's a little boy, almost hidden in the crowd, who is saying that he has seen a big white flash coming down from the sky almost like a bird. No one seems to know for certain, however; and as there are no more people for washing the crowd begins to drift away.

---

[100] John 12:26

Like John who baptised him, we puzzle over the reason for Jesus' baptism. Jesus has not done anything wrong, so we don't know why he had to be washed clean in baptism like all the rest of us who have certainly sinned and done wrong. But we can learn a lot from looking at that film as it were of Jesus' baptism and noticing one particular detail. At the moment of his baptism the waters of the Jordan closed over Jesus' head, and he was then on a lower level than everybody around him. Now, we call Jesus our King but we see from that incident that he was no King of Siam, demanding that no one's head be higher than his own. Jesus' kingship did not consist of outward display or rank – Jesus was not worried that everybody was looking down upon him beneath the waters of the Jordan: he knew what he had to do, and he was ready to do it, no matter what other people's views were.

"Where I am, there shall also my servant be." An important message there for the institutional Church. I have been saddened over the years to read reports of conferences which re-affirmed "the value of the laity". I have also read the Archbishop of Canterbury's comment that it is his firm conviction that "the laity hold the key to the advancement of the kingdom", and it is his hope that "we should learn how best to release their huge potential".[101]

I could not help thinking what a pompous and patronising view of the laity those clerical words reveal. The laity does not hold the "keys to the advancement of God's kingdom": the laity is that key. However, we must be very careful how we use the word "laity". "Laity" has overtones of ignorance and inexperience, and when the clergy use that word it is all too easy for him or her to forget that he or she also is a member of the laity, a member of the *laos*, the Greek word from which we derive "laity" and which means the people of God. Moreover, the clergy as clergyman or clergywoman are not very important members of the people of God,

---

[101] George Carey, Archbishop of Canterbury from 1991 to 2002. Quote from his 1992 Christmas message.

158

whatever his or her dignity. How can we the clergy be all that important? We are simply the enablers, the resource people, channels of God's grace to the world, to whom the other members of the *laos*, the people of God, turn, we hope, for help in confronting the world with the message of God – and proclaiming God in the world is what it's all about, not being a member of the ordained ministry.

All my life I have fought against the phrase "he went into the Church" to describe what happened at my ordination. I was already in the Church before I was ordained. My baptism took me into the Church and made me a member of the people of God; and my membership of the people of God is far more important to me than the fact of my ordination.

It's such a pity, I sometimes think, that we clergy wear swell clothes in church, move about in solemn procession, and climb up on high to address you because it becomes all too easy for us to lay the law down. One fact is we wear different clothes to emphasise the age-long continuity of what the Church is about. We move in procession because we have to get from A to B and back again, and think we ought to do so in a seemly fashion; and we climb into the pulpit to speak to you because it is easier for you if you can see us as well as hear us.

Contrary to appearances, therefore, we clergy are not all that important. We are important only in so far as we are, to borrow one of the Bishop of Rome's titles, servants of the servants of God. Baptism makes a person a servant of God: ordination makes a person a servant of the servants of God. To be a servant of God, to advance God's kingdom in the world is far more exciting, far more dangerous, far more important than being a mere servant of the servants of God, serving in the second line.

If people take a higher view of the clergy than they ought, are they right in their opinion of the whole Church of which the clergy are such a small part? If I can believe my non-Christian friends and my friends of other churches or denominations, the Church of England is not highly regarded. "An exclusive social club the members of which aren't really interested in anybody else." "People who meet together for mutual moral uplift which does not issue in any positive outside action." Those are two types of reactions. Perhaps, in all humility, we ought to be asking ourselves, what effect we, the worshipping baptised, are having upon our immediate neighbourhood – what effect for God?

We, the baptised, are the servants of God, and we serve God as we serve his world. We cannot serve God's world unless we're prepared to be humble, and not bothered about what others may think of us. To change the metaphor, we have to be ready to get our hands dirty for other people. We can all think of times when we didn't because we were scared of what people might think.

"Where I am, there shall also my servant be", and Jesus was consistent in where he was. He began his ministry by allowing people to look down upon him beneath the waters of baptism. At the end of his life, in the upper room, at supper with his friends for the last time, he knelt before them to wash their dirty feet. Doubtless they looked down upon him in love and wonder as he did so. But even if they'd looked down in contempt and disdain that he was stooping to such a service, it wouldn't have mattered – Jesus would still have washed their feet.

We have been baptised into God's service, and we serve him best as we serve his world. If people look down upon us as we do so it does not matter – *"Where I am, there shall also my servant be"*.

The ministry of the laity

The Sunday before Christmas Day has traditionally been one of the four normal occasions on which there take place ordinations to the sacred ministry of the Church. The week before is therefore kept as a time of special prayer for ordinands. Also, the words of the collect for the third Sunday in Advent[102] as provided for in the Book of Common Prayer

---

[102] O Lord Jesus Christ, who at thy first coming didst send thy messenger to prepare thy way before thee: Grant that the ministers

appear to be directed towards the same topic – they speak of "the ministers and stewards of God's mysteries". When most people hear these words, they immediately think of the members of the ordained ministry. The confusion arises because we are all, whether we've been ordained or not, we are all, in a very real sense, ministers; or to put it another way, we all have a ministry to perform.

"Am I my brother's keeper?"[103] By asking that question Cain tried to disassociate himself from his brother Abel's murder. We may not put Cain's question in exactly the same way but there's no denying that we often try to make the same point, when we try to shuffle out of any real responsibility for the well-being of our fellow human beings. But all those of us who respond to God's call and become members of the Church have, individually and corporately, a great responsibility towards our fellows. As members of the Church, we are members of the body of people chosen to proclaim the gospel, to be messengers to prepare God's way, to be Christians. Isaiah, in Old Testament times, and, in New Testament times, John Baptist, both interpreted the preparation of God's way as the making of it smooth and the taking away of the obstacles and difficulties which are so often in its path.

Members of the ordained ministry cannot, by themselves alone, prepare God's way adequately. Suppose every single parishioner in a parish to be an active practising Christian. The poor clergy would then be more than run off their feet – so many babies to be baptised, so many Holy Communions to be celebrated, so many people to marry, and prepare for marriage, so many dead to bury and bereaved to comfort, so many confessions to be heard, so much spiritual direction to be given, so many sick to have the laying on of hands and to

---

and stewards of thy mysteries may likewise so prepare and make ready thy way, by turning the hearts of the disobedient to the wisdom of the just, that at thy second coming to judge the world we may be found an acceptable people in thy sight, who liveth and reigneth with the Father, the Holy Spirit; ever one God world without end. Amen.

[103] Genesis 4:9

be visited, not to mention patiently listening to all the problems people stumble over as they try to walk the way back to God.

It is perhaps a good thing that so few parishioners take the Christian faith seriously, though we may be sure that if more were to do so God would call sufficient numbers to the sacred ministry to cope with the situation. But the problem actually facing us is that of persuading the vast majority of parishioners to take us seriously: that is a problem that the clergy cannot tackle at all successfully on their own. Visiting and getting to know every single parishioner is a time-consuming business. It's a traditional ideal for the parson to get to know all his or her parishioners; but it has to be more honoured in the breach than the observance. I tried to carry it out myself when I was an incumbent in Norfolk, and found that it left me little time for anything else – and all the while I had to leave off and answer other legitimate and important calls on my time. Nor did I find that a home-going parson made for an immediately churchgoing people.

The business of preparing the way of the Lord has, therefore, to be looked at again. The clergy cannot tackle it with much hope of success, for reasons already given - there are so few of them, and they should be more than busy doing other things, such things as their ordination service refers to. It may help to picture a parish on the map as a circle, more or less. In the centre of the circle is the parish church to which we come to worship God, to learn more about God, to deepen our faith and trust in him and to study his ways. In fact, we cannot be good Christians if we are not good members of the Church. But it's also true that we are not good Christians if all we do is come to church. What we have to do, to be truly and fully Christian, all of us, is to go out of the church after worship and spread the good news, proclaim the gospel, wherever we find ourselves, and wherever it seems the right moment to do so. The technique's not a new one: the communists have been very good at it in recent times, and some of today's cults are successful with it, but the Church seems largely to have forgotten it - the technique of instruction in lots of small groups whose members are then dispersed to make as many believers as possible.

It's everybody's job to be Christ's agent, Christ's ambassador, Christ's representative. It is not a job the clergy can do with much success, there being so few of them, to make the point yet again. But if all of us, all the baptised that is, look upon ourselves as God's agents all the time, and model our behaviour and speech accordingly, they will be so very many more of us to help make ready the way of the Lord, to turn the hearts of the disobedient to the wisdom of the just. And we do not have to become Bible-punchers in order to prepare the way of the Lord, nor do we have to climb up on some religious soapbox. The quickest way may be the best way – regular weekly worship with the rest of the Christian community, daily Bible-reading, trying sincerely to live our daily lives as God would have us live them, always ready to allow others to see how important God is to us. Remember: the little things matter as much as the big things. It may be some small thing that prevents the love of God shining into our hearts; and it may be some little thing that we do that makes all the difference to some fellow-traveller on the path of life.

Preparing the way of the Lord is too important to be left to the clergy alone, quite apart from the fact that there are not enough of them to do it properly, even if it were one of their first priorities. But it is not – the job of the clergy is to help and support the baptised in spreading the good news. As baptised themselves, the clergy will do what they can to proclaim the gospel; but, as clergy, theirs is a more particular task, to guide and enable the whole people of God, those who have made a commitment to Christ, to turn the hearts of the disobedient to the wisdom of the just.

Wrong things are expected of both clergy and non-clergy alike – that's why the Church seems so inadequate a tool in God's hands today. "*Seek ye first the kingdom of God.*"[104] We must seek God first before we can look at the world

---

[104] Matthew 6:33

properly. When we see God first, then we shall know what to do, and know that the job of the clergy is important, and that of the non-clergy is equally, if not more, important. If we do not have the vision, the clergy will be undervalued, and the non-clergy will fail to realise what it is they're supposed to be doing, proclaiming the gospel, spreading the good news.

What is the job of a priest?

Habemus papam. We have a Pope – well-known words spoken from a famous balcony, the balcony of St Peter's Church in Rome, when a new pope is presented to the faithful.

The election of a new pope, the appointment of a new vicar, should make us think about what a priest is for, what is the job of a priest? We can see the beginnings of an answer in the service of Holy Communion. The priest will go to the altar and there set out the mystery of God's love for us in the holy bread and wine of the sacrament of the altar.

The sacraments are God's free gifts to us: and they are most lovely gifts, the most precious gifts ever. In the sacraments God gives himself to us. The sacraments do not depend on anything special in those who receive them: no-one can earn them. Nor do the sacraments depend on anything special about the priest, except that he or she is a priest.

There's nothing random or haphazard about the sacraments. They do not come down to us like rain from heaven. The sacraments come from the great tree as it were of apostolic ministry. Christ planted that tree when he called twelve men and made them his ambassadors: and that tree has grown immensely huge – it spreads its arms over all the earth. Ordination is what grafts every new priest onto that tree.

Priests are living branches on the great tree of apostolic ministry, bearing sacraments as its fruit. At the altar, the priest gives us the body and blood of Christ. When we make our confession, the priest gives us Christ's absolution.

164

When we are ill, and when we are about to die, the priest may anoint us with Christ's soothing and healing oil. The priest is present to solemnise men and women joining themselves together in holy matrimony and to give them Christ's blessing.

Priests not only give us the sacraments. Someone once said that a priest is a walking sacrament, an appointed flag for Christians to rally around, a centre of unity to hold Christians together in any one place, a minister not only of the sacraments but of the word of God also – it was a wise Roman Catholic priest who said that he is only half a priest who does not know how to break the bread of the word to his people.

Being a priest is terrifying. No other calling shows people up as much as the priesthood does. Nothing prevents a priest from being a very ordinary person. Being a priest does not, in itself, make us kinder or wiser or more experienced than anyone else. What being a priest does do is give our fellow Christians a right to our services.

The woman next door may be better at teaching than the local schoolteacher. But that does not mean we may call upon her to teach our little ones – that's the job of the schoolteacher. It is the same with priests: you have a right to our services – use us, therefore, as much as you like, so long as it's to fulfil genuine needs for the specific services of a priest. Anyone may be a better Christian than a priest, more holy, more full of prayer. Anyone may be more learned than the priest. But priests do have the special duty and obligation to pray and to learn about God. Other people may be better at speaking about Christ, but priests must speak about Christ; priests must feed their flock with God's word.

What priests stand for is therefore infinitely greater than themselves. But, when we come to think about it, that is true of every Christian, whether ordained priest or not. Everyone has to be a Christopher, a Christ-bearer. Whoever we are, we are, each one of us without exception, pygmies, little people: but when we put on the armour of God then we become a force to be reckoned with in this wicked world.

The army of the baptised people of God is the best army there has ever been or will be.

Thank God that he does not wait for anyone of us to become perfect. God is always making himself available, accessible. He is presenting himself to us in the holy bread and wine of the altar. Whenever we avail ourselves of them, God makes a gift of himself to us in all the other sacraments. God is always there for us – after all, he gave himself to us as a helpless child crying in a manger. He allowed himself to be manhandled most cruelly for our sakes as he was nailed to a piece of wood. God is always here for us: let us worship and adore him.

The activities of a priest

There is a story told about a certain monastery, which is quite amusing. That monastery had it laid down as one of its rules that all its monks had to hear a sermon on every Sunday of the year. Now you may say that there is nothing surprising about that, except that it shows that monks are not, after all, so very different from us if they have to be ordered to hear a sermon. But the point about the rule which is interesting is this: although the monks were ordered to hear a sermon on every Sunday of the year there was one Sunday on which they escaped a sermon, and that Sunday was Trinity Sunday. The reason why they were let off a sermon on this Sunday was because the subject for a sermon most suitable, that of God the Holy Trinity, is such a difficult subject for a preacher to talk about.

Fortunately for us, however, Trinity Sunday, is also one of the occasions in the year in which men and women are ordained to the ministry of the Church, and so, although I cannot shelter under the monastic role forbidding a sermon, I can, equally suitably, talk to you about the nature and functions of the ministry, which may be a somewhat easier task than the task of tackling the mystery of God's nature and being. For we see, as we move about in our daily lives, men and women dressed in a distinctive garb: their collars are worn back to front, in the performance of their duties they wear a long black robe, or it may be a purple one. We ask ourselves, therefore, what sort of job is it which these men and women are doing? Of what number, and of what sort of activities does it consist?

If we look at the Book of Common Prayer, we shall find that there are three main activities in which the ministers of the Church engage. They are firstly the administration of the sacraments, secondly the preaching of the Word, thirdly the giving of spiritual counsel and advice.

First, the administration of the sacraments. The sacraments should be administered frequently for they are the appointed gateways between heaven and earth. Through them, the life of God moves into the world of men and women and men and women may pass through them into the life of heaven. Administration of the sacraments will, therefore, take up a great deal of a priest's time and energy. Certain of the sacraments, for example holy baptism, may be administered once only in a person's life. In the case of holy matrimony, the Church of England hopes it will occur only once within a person's lifetime. However, it is important to remember that not everyone gets married, just as not everyone feels the call to be ordained. But the administering of Holy Communion, both in church and in the homes of those who are not able to make their way to church, should take place not once only, whether it be once a year, once a month, or once a week, but as often and as frequently as our souls feel the need for it – and who can tell how often we should feel the need for the help and the strength which come to us from God through the Holy Communion?

Administration of the sacraments is, therefore, one of the first activities to which a priest is called. The priest is called by God not for any worldly qualities of popularity or likeableness which he or she may possess but simply to be an instrument, the means by which God's grace may come into the world as he or she administers the sacraments. And so, it matters not one jot, for example, whether we like our priests or not, not even whether we approve of their way of living. What does matter is that they have been appointed by God to convey his strength and comfort to work through the sacraments which they alone can administer. We have therefore no excuse for not going to this or that church because we cannot get on with this or that priest. The important fact about a priest is that he or she has been appointed to administer to us the sacraments through which alone we can be absolutely certain of being in touch with God.

The second activity to which a priest is called is to preach the Word. It is one of the glories of the Church of England that she holds the preaching of the Word and the administration of the sacraments in equal balance, the one being no more important in her system for Christian living than the other. But the importance which the Church of England attaches to the preaching of the Word should not be judged from the number of sermons which are currently being preached in the churches of our land. Surprising as this may sound, we learn just how important the Church of England regards preaching when we read that on only one occasion on a Sunday does she expect a sermon to be preached, and that at a celebration of the Holy Eucharist. We have become so accustomed to having a sermon at Morning and Evening Prayer that it comes as a shock to us to discover that we should, strictly speaking, have only one sermon on a Sunday, and that during the Communion Service.

The reason behind that ruling of our Church is the well-known but often forgotten maxim, that quantity is no substitute for quality. The saying of an old English clergyman is as true today as it was when he uttered it: – "if I preach thrice on Sundays I prate – speak foolishly – twice". For to preach a sermon which is worthy of the name requires a great deal of time and energy. It requires not only the time and energy which are used in the composing of it. It requires a solid background of regular and frequent study of the Bible, for example. That study, a promise to be diligent in which, was obtained from each candidate for the priesthood with the upmost solemnity at his or her ordination.

Unfortunately, however, there are ever so many things which take much of the time which the priest should be devoting to his or her study of the Scriptures. Administrative jobs, keeping the parish machinery running smoothly and in good order, visiting newcomers to the parish – those are perhaps some of the jobs which should be undertaken by the members of our congregation, thus freeing the priest for that study of the Bible without which he or she will fail in his vocation.

The third activity in which the ministers of the Church engage themselves is one which is sadly neglected in the Church of England today. This is largely because people do not obey a most important direction which is found within the pages of the Book of Common Prayer, because – tragically enough for the life and effectiveness of our Church – people do not even know of that direction, that direction which is to be found towards the end of the first exhortation which is appointed to be read during the service of Holy Communion, the direction to go to a priest for spiritual counsel and advice.

I do not believe that there is a single one of us who can honestly say that alone and without the help of another they can overcome all the difficulties which they encounter on their way back to God. Sermons are all very well, but they give us only the general principles of the Christian life and it is left to the individual to apply those principles in the daily circumstances of his or her life, which is not always as easy to do as you may think.

Nor can it be said that we receive all the help which we need through our prayers, when we listen hard for God's guiding voice. It is on this very point that the protestant and catholic traditions within the Church are agreeing more and more. For the catholic way of life has always held that it is right and proper to discuss with another the details of our prayer life. Hear now what an eminent Swiss protestant has to say about it: "it is important above all to share with a friend all ideas about what has happened to us in the period of silent meditation... Without something like that, a quiet time for myself alone would frequently be a mere self-contemplation. Such discussion becomes the surest means of differentiating between our own ideas and God's will, of separating the wheat from the chaff." Translate that into the language used towards the end of the first exhortation in the communion service and you will see that both the Swiss protestant and the Anglican exhortation are making the same point – use a priest for spiritual counsel and advice.

Those then are three activities to which a priest is called. Frequent and regular administration of the sacraments in which alone we can certainly share in the life of heaven whilst here on earth. Preaching of the Word which requires long and diligent study of the Scriptures. The giving of spiritual counsel and advice which is sorely needed within the life of our Church today. Pray for your priests, therefore, both for those who are newly ordained in the sacred ministry and for those who have already been in it for some time. Pray for them that they may ever be faithful to their calling. And pray also for more priests to be raised up within our land that our land may become the home of a truly Christian nation.

The priest's ability to forgive sins

It is amazing what a great challenge can be presented to us in the use of a single word. Matthew 9:8 ends with the word "men". "*They marvelled, and glorified God, who had given such power and unto men*". But the passage in which that sentence occurs describes only one man to whom such power had been given. Jesus, and no one else, had healed the sick of the palsy and forgiven his sins. The question arises, therefore, why the end of the passage speaks of men while the beginning of the passage mentions only one man. There must have been a very good reason why St Matthew, the author of the passage, turned his mind from thinking of Jesus as exercising the power to forgive sins to thinking of other people as also possessing that power. When we have discovered that reason, we shall find that it presents us with a challenge. The challenge, what use do you make of your priests?

The reason for the discrepancy in St Matthew's story is the value which the early Church placed upon the priest's power to forgive sins. St Matthew was recounting the story about Jesus' power to forgive sins. But, together with his fellow members of the early Church, St Matthew believed that Jesus had passed on that power to his priests, and the priests' exercise of that power and the lasting benefits which that confers were looming so large in St Matthew's mind that a slip of his tongue has been recorded for ever. The slip of his tongue was this. St Matthew began a story about Jesus' power to forgive sins, a power which he had in his own right as God, a power which brought indescribable comfort and joy to men, not least to the sick of palsy. As he was setting down the story, St Matthew's mind wandered away from Jesus' power to forgive sins, which brought so much healing into the world, to the wholesome exercise of that same power by the priests to whom Jesus had delegated it. Perhaps St Matthew had experienced for himself the benefit of going to confession, as we call it today, and that was why he slipped into using the plural word "men" where, strictly speaking, he should have used the singular word "man", referring to Jesus.

St Matthew was not the only person to know the value of confession of sins to a priest or their forgiveness by him or her. Some of the first candidates for holy baptism were told of its importance. They were required to say, "I believe in the forgiveness of sins". It is unlikely that forgiveness of sins would have been mentioned so early in the creed if the priest's power to forgive sins had not played a large part in the daily lives of those first Christians. Almost from the beginning of her history, therefore, the Church has believed that Jesus passes on to his priests the power to pronounce in his name and authority forgiveness of sins, that power which Jesus possesses by right of being God. The words which priests of today utter as they pronounce the forgiveness of sins after hearing a confession shows that the Church still

171

holds that belief – those words are, "by his authority committed to me I absolve thee from all thy sins".

It is easy to pile proof upon proof that, throughout the ages, the Church has seen in the priest an image of Christ's power to forgive sins. Ambrose, Bishop of Milan from 374A.D. onwards, refused to allow the Emperor Theodosius to make his communion in the cathedral until Theodosius had confessed the sin which he had committed in a notorious massacre of men and women at Thessalonica. In that incident we see the priest's power of forgiving sins together with the priest's authority to rebuke sins, an authority which our Book of Common Prayer allows to the priest, in the rubric to be found at the beginning of the Holy Communion service: "if any be an open and notorious evil doer, or have done any wrong to his neighbours by word or deed, so that the congregation is thereby offended; a curate, having knowledge of thereof, shall call him and advertise him, that in any wise he presume not to come to the Lord's table, until he have openly declared himself to have truly repented and amended his former naughty life, that the congregation may thereby be satisfied, which before were offended; that he have recompensed the parties, to whom he had done wrong; or at least declare himself to be in full purpose so to do, as soon as he conveniently may."

But we must not emphasise the disciplinary aspect of the priest's power to forgive sins at the cost of neglecting its healing aspect. Jesus healed the sick of the palsy bodily and spiritually, but it is amazing what a difference may be made to the health of our whole person if we avail ourselves of the priest's power to forgive sins. "If" we avail ourselves. For at no time has our Church laid it down that every single member of it must go to confession. The Anglican golden rule about confession is that "all may, no one must, some should". The question which each one of us has to ask themself is, therefore, the question, should not I make use of my priests in the way in which Jesus has made it possible for me to use them and in which all the whole Church has always used them? If anybody finds it difficult to answer that question let them read in the Book of Common Prayer the words of the long exhortation which is to be found after the prayer for the Church militant: "if there be any of you, who by this means cannot quiet his own conscience, but requireth further comfort or counsel, let him come to me or to some other discreet and learned minister of God's word, and open his grief; but by ministry of God's holy word he may receive the benefit of absolution, together with ghostly counsel and advice, to the quieting of his conscience, and avoiding of all scruple and doubtfulness".

"*They marvelled, and glorified God, who had given such power unto men.*"[105] The last word of that sentence contains a challenge, the challenge, what use do you make of your priests? Among the other uses which you make of your priests do not forget that they have been given the power to forgive you your sins.

Questions for discussion or reflection

- *Reflecting on the role of the priest, in summary, to administer the sacraments, preach the Word and to provide spiritual counsel and guidance, how do you "use" your priest? Are there any ways in which you should make better use of your priest?*

- *Do you have any outward sign to show that you are a Christian? If so, what is it and why do you have it?*

- *Explain the ways in which you are an ambassador of Christ. How does your priest enable you to fulfil this role?*

---

[105] Matthew 9:8

SD - #0045 - 151221 - C0 - 216/138/10 - PB - 9781913181680 - Gloss Lamination